THE
GREAT HOUSES
OF PARIS

An Hachette-Vendome Book

Designed by Pierre Faucheux

THE GREAT HOUSES OF PARIS

Claude Frégnac and Wayne Andrews

with a preface by Jacques Wilhelm
Honorary Chief Curator, Musée Carnavalet, Paris

The Vendome Press
New York   Paris   Lausanne

Translation from the French by James Emmons
Design consultant: Marlene Rothkin Vine

Copyright © 1977 by Librairie Hachette, Paris
Copyright © 1979 English adaptation by The Vendome Press, New York
First published in Great Britain by Weidenfeld and Nicolson Limited

Library of Congress Catalog Card Number: 79–5094

ISBN 0–670–34972–0

Printed and bound in Italy

Preface

The fine series of historic houses illustrated in this book range in date from the late 15th century to the Second Empire (1852–70). All these structures bear the name *hôtel*, which in medieval France would have designated either a royal residence or the mansion of any man of rank or wealth. Pre-Renaissance Paris could boast only one *palace*, that of the King on the Île de la Cité, where the Roman overlords of ancient Gaul had established their *palatium*. The Louvre being a fortified castle, the Hôtel Saint-Pol in the shadow of the Bastille served as the town house to which King Charles V (1364–80) withdrew for privacy, relaxation, and amusement.

Time and circumstance have changed the meaning of these terms. When its towers were demolished, the Louvre became a palace, like the Luxembourg, the residence of a French Queen born in Italy (Marie de' Medici). Sheer size seems to have required that the term "palace" be applied to the Palais-Cardinal (the mansion of Cardinal Richelieu, which, when he gave it to the King, became the Palais-Royal), to the Palais Bourbon, to the Palais Soubise, and later, under the Third Republic, to the Palais Rose. Perhaps it was in imitation of Renaissance Italy that so often in France a fine mansion came to be thought of as a palace. But, with a few exceptions, the Parisian town houses never approached the size and extent of the great Roman *palazzi*.

It was not size that caused a private town house to be known as an *hôtel*, but rather its owner's rank. As late as the mid-17th century, *hôtel* distinguished the homes of the nobility from those of wealthy commoners, of magistrates and financiers, even when the latter had been more or less recently ennobled by the purchase of an office or estate. The mansion of a great commoner like Ragois de Bretonvilliers, though one of the largest houses in Paris, or that of the magistrate Lambert de Thorigny, a little smaller but equally magnificent, was referred to as *maison* ("house"). *Hôtel* seemed appropriate only for the homes of the old aristocracy. Richelet's French dictionary of 1680 defines *hôtel* as "the house of a lord of quality." But already this had become an archaism. In the reign of Louis XIV (1643–1715) the distinction between *maison* and *hôtel* gradually evaporated, and henceforth in common parlance the word *hôtel* went to designate any town house enhanced by a carriage gateway, stables, and coach houses, and occupied by a single family, whether of the nobility or the bourgeoisie.

To build an *hôtel* worthy of the name was at all times a costly undertaking. It had to last for generations. Yet in Paris the remaining *hôtels* of the 15th and 16th centuries can be counted on one's fingers, while several cities in Italy still possess dozens of *palazzi* dating to the Middle Ages and

5

the Renaissance. This can be explained by the fact that in France, down to the reign of Louis XIII (1610–43), most of the nobility lived on their country estates. Only the great nobles who attended the monarch and followed him from *château* to *château* maintained residences of their own in Paris. But the mansions belonging to Princes of the blood and members of the greatest families were large and luxurious indeed. So were those built by the Italian bankers or favorites who followed the Medici Queens to Paris—men like Adjacet, Gondi, or Concini. The other *hôtels* of the French Renaissance and the reign of Henri IV (1589–1610) assumed a much smaller scale.

The bourgeoisie, as the name indicates, lived in town. From its upper class, rich enough to purchase high offices and rise to noble rank, came the great magistrates. Other affluent commoners found it possible to enrich themselves as tax collectors, bankers, businessmen, building contractors, and real estate speculators, while the old nobility grew steadily poorer, drawing a fixed income from their estates and spending it on war and fine display at court. The new *hôtels* of the bourgeoisie were not always built on unoccupied ground, and all too often older houses were pulled down to make way for them. The French have been described as conservatives who destroy; but the rich of every period want their splendid houses to reflect the style of the day.

The wars of religion in the 16th century checked private construction, but afterwards, for that very reason, new building flourished in the time of Louis XIII and down to the death of Cardinal Mazarin (1661). Then, however, until the end of the 17th century, little was built, the compulsion to live at court under Louis XIV at Versailles being too great. Moreover, the old nobility had their ancestral homes and felt no need of new ones. They were not attracted to the Place Royale (now Place des Vosges) until later, when the grandees could be sure of finding themselves in good company there. The first of the fine houses in the Place Royale were built by middleclass speculators, who sold or let them to high magistrates or great nobles. Likewise, when the Île Saint-Louis came under development in the late 17th century, it attracted chiefly magistrates, financiers, plain citizens, and even artisans.

Those with newly made fortunes had every reason to build, for property investments yielded a good return. Furthermore, the *nouveaux riches* were intent on "showing off," on giving luster to their new titles, and making a good match for their children. La Bruyère, writing in the 1680s, describes one Périandre: "His house is superb. The Doric order reigns in its imposing exterior: this is not a doorway, it is a portal. But could this be called a private house or a temple? Common people take it for the latter. [The owner] is the lord of the whole neighborhood."

Gruyn des Bordes, a tavern-keeper's son, reaped immense profits as an army contractor and built the Hôtel Lauzun. Many businessmen at that time accumulated unprecedented riches. In the 1660s, after the death of Mazarin, Colbert, Louis XIV's great finance minister, complained that "buildings, furniture, silverplate, and ornaments are a monopoly of the men of high finance, who spend prodigious sums on them." The wealthy Samuel Bernard, unusual in being a Protestant, began as a small linen-draper. After the revocation of the Edict of Nantes (1685), he acted as Paris correspondent for exiled Protestants and lived in a town house in the Place des Victoires. By the end of the reign of Louis XIV (1715), he was the richest man in France and lent money to the crown. Early in the reign of Louis XV (1715–74), Peyrenc de Moras, a former hairdresser, built the finest town house in the Faubourg Saint-Germain—today the Rodin Museum. The great nobles did not disdain these parvenus. That is, they did not disdain their money, for by marrying the latter's daughters, they too could build fine houses.

The creation of these *hôtels* was a key factor in the expansion of Paris. It must not be forgotten that the great houses always stood side by side with the dwellings of the middle and lower classes. They were not built on the Île de la Cité, nor in the district of the Halles (central markets) on the right bank, nor in that of the University on the left bank. They appeared on fresh land extending out from the old heart of the city. This occurred, first of all, on the east side where in the late Middle Ages the Hôtel Saint-Pol and the Hôtel des Tournelles had attracted courtiers and officials. One of these royal residences was demolished under François I (1515–47), and the other after the accidental death of Henri II (1547–59). Where they had stood, regular streets were introduced and the Place Royale was laid out, the latter becoming by the mid-17th century the center of social life in the Marais quarter. The development of the Île Saint-Louis was part of this movement eastwards from the Cité. But the old nobility had many residences on the west side, around the Louvre, near which Cardinal Richelieu erected his palace. In the new streets of that neighborhood lived the great ministers Mazarin and Colbert; and there, even after Louis XIV had left Paris for Versailles, such ministers as Louvois, Pontchartrain, and Chamillart built their homes.

The district north of the Halles was devoted to business and, as early as the 13th century, to banking, its indispensable mainstay. There, in the time of Louis XIII (1610–43), lived the high aristocracy, ministers, financiers, and the great tax collectors known as "farmers-general." The laying out of the Place des Victoires in the late 17th century, then of the Place Vendôme, marked two stages in the westward movement. Contemporaries noted that all the sumptuous town houses erected around the Place Vendôme, with superb façades designed by Jules Hardouin-Mansart, belonged to "rich men who have made fortunes out of the late wars and thus acquired the means of living like lords." The new *hôtels* belonged, that is, to army contractors and financiers. Those in the Faubourg Saint-Honoré, then open country, arose around the town house of the Comte d'Évreux. Now the Palais de l'Élysée, residence of the President of the Republic, this great mansion was built with money acquired by the Comte d'Évreux through his marriage to the daughter of the rich financier, Antoine Crozat.

On the left bank the Palais du Luxembourg, built in 1615–20 by Marie de' Medici, Henri IV's widowed Queen, was soon surrounded by other mansions. The development of the Pré-aux-Clercs led to the laying out of long streets running parallel to the Seine, streets that gradually came to be lined with magnificent houses with extensive gardens, which, in the course of the 18th century, would reach as far as the Invalides. For a long time, almost to the present day, this quarter retained its residential and patrician character. In the late reign of Louis XV (1715–74) and under Louis XVI (1774–92), Paris spread northwards, into the zone of the present boulevards, and steadily westwards, while the Marais to the east was gradually deserted by people of fashion.

The French Revolution drove the owners from most of these fine houses, emptied many of them of their treasures, and put the premises to strange and unexpected uses. Cannon balls, for instance, were cast in the Hôtel de Bretonvilliers, and the mansion of the Maréchal de Richelieu in the Rue d'Antin was turned into a dance hall. When order returned, those who had lived in the old town houses preferred to take up residence in new and different quarters. It was then that the *hôtels* of the Marais, the Temple, and the Richelieu districts were taken over by artisans and tradesmen, and their courtyards and gardens covered with sheds, warehouses, and workshops. The great interior spaces were divided up into apartments and filled with humble tenants, who often found themselves living under ceilings richly painted with soaring, illusionistic scenes of airborne mythological events. During the 19th century some of the pre-Revolution town houses in the eastern districts became the homes of artists and writers. In the Place des Vosges, Victor Hugo lived in the Hôtel de Chaulnes. Meanwhile, the novelist Alphonse Daudet moved into the Hôtel de Lamoignon, and the poets Théophile Gautier and Charles Baudelaire into the Hôtel Lauzun on the Île Saint-Louis.

Returning from exile after 1815, the old legitimist nobility settled on the left bank in the Faubourg Saint-Germain. There Balzac situated the town houses of the Vicomtesse de Beauséant, the Duchesse de Langeais, and the Duchesse de Maufrigneuse, while Madame de Restaud, old Goriot's daughter, lived in the Rue du Helder and her sister, wife of the banker Nucingen, in the Rue Saint-Lazare. The financiers reclaimed their hold on the boulevards, the Chaussée d'Antin, and the Faubourg Saint-Honoré, where, in the course of the 19th century, the Rothschilds, leaving the Rue Laffitte, gradually ventured out from the Place de la Concorde to the Avenue de Marigny.

Under the Second Empire (1852–70), the Pereire brothers parceled out one-half of the Parc Monceau, the former "English garden" of the Duc d'Orléans, and some extraordinary residences rose there along a series of short avenues. Others, aristocratic or middleclass, were built along the Champs-Élysées, around the Place de l'Étoile, and, under the Third Republic (1870–1940), along the fine avenues of the 16th Arrondissement—Neuilly and Auteuil—which then became a fashionable neighborhood, in the direction of the Bois de Boulogne. It was then that in French usage a private town house came to be called, not simply *hôtel*, but *hôtel particulier*, to distinguish it from a house for the accommodation of travelers.

From the time of the Second Empire onward, many town houses, mainly the new ones, were redecorated to imitate the styles of the past; or the paneling and even painted ceilings were removed from old, decaying mansions and reinstalled in recently built ones. After World War I many of the greatest town houses went on the market, being too expensive to maintain, or suffered conversion to other purposes. The few new ones erected in the past fifty years near the Bois de Boulogne all belong to wealthy foreigners.

The Parisian town house was always an essential element of the urban setting, in harmony with the architectural style of its street and neighborhood. In the Middle Ages it took sinuous forms and was adorned with a superstructure, more symbolic than effective, of battlements and pepper-pot turrets. During the Renaissance *hôtels* followed a more regular design, as can still be seen in remains of the Louis XIII period. While the principal front of Italian *palazzi* stands flush with the street, the Parisian town house of the classical period has only its formal entrance on the street, at the center of a secondary building or a wall connecting the lodges at either end of the wings. The foreward structures shield the *corps de logis,* or actual house, which sits well back on the far side of the courtyard with its longest façade giving onto the garden behind. Above the low walls separating the enclosure from the gardens of adjacent houses, the trees mingle their leafage, forming a haven of peace where the inhabitants of these privileged places are sheltered from the noise and promiscuity of the street. Around the former royal squares, however, and along the embankments of the Île Saint-Louis, the town houses do have their main fronts directly on the street, so that from the state apartments on the *premier étage* (really the second story) one has a view of the river or, on the squares, of the fine architectural ensembles around them. In the old days the occupants could view the pageants and processions that continuously unfolded in the open space below.

A large, roomy building, with courtyard and garden and various outbuildings, sometimes with an orange-greenhouse, was the home of the master and mistress and their family, waited on by a staff of several dozen servants. Privacy generally had to be sacrificed to a life of permanent display, for which these noble, high-ceilinged rooms were designed, all opening into each other at first and having a double exposure, then from the mid-17th century laid out somewhat more conveniently. The very size and height of the main building made it possible to fit out smaller, more intimate rooms, in addition to the state apartments. The latter included the drawing room, the anterooms where dinner was often served, the main hall or state room, sometimes two stories high in the Italian manner, and, in the more majestic mansions, the gallery or long room which soon gave way to the drawing room, before being replaced finally by the parlor

Since guests were usually received in the state room, a side room often served as a bedroom and, with its adjoining study or closet (ancestor of the boudoir) and chapel or oratory, constituted the nucleus of a more private apartment. Under Louis XIV, it was still very unusual for any particular room to be set aside as a proper dining room, even though it was the custom in great houses to keep open board. When receptions were held, the neighboring streets filled with carriages, and the host of footmen waiting on their masters crowded into the entrance hall and the first anteroom. The members of well-to-do families, often having little else to do, called on each other daily, and the continual round of visits from one town house to another is vividly described in the letters of Madame de Sévigné (1626–96).

The splendor of the interior décor accorded fully with this grand style of living. The anterooms were covered with embossed leather or hung with tapestries, velvet, or silk. In the finest houses the state room and the gallery had wainscoting and wood-paneled walls, painted, often on a gold ground, with flowers, arabesques, and mythological scenes, all set out in keeping with a precise iconographic program. Under Louis XIII (1610–43), the ceilings exposed their beams; a little later they bore coffers; by the middle of the century they began to be painted with gods and goddesses in an airy, *trompe l'oeil* setting of sky and clouds. About 1680, these elaborate decorations gave way to paneling painted white and gold, or covered over in other uniform colors, subdued or bright. Now painted ceilings went out of fashion, not to reappear until the Neoclassical period.

In the 18th century carved woodwork formed the usual decoration of elegant town houses, some of which, as a supreme luxury, contained furniture specially designed for a particular room or setting. But few of these fine ensembles of period furniture or woodwork have survived. Even more rare are early 19th-century townhouses in which can yet be found the original décor of painted grotesques in the Pompeiian style; rarer still the town houses of the Second Empire which retain the polychrome marbles and sculptured ornaments so characteristic of that flamboyant era. The fine tapestries, moreover, that set them off have survived only in the most exceptional instance.

While the abandonment of certain neighborhoods by the great families who lived there before the Revolution led to much destruction and havoc, paradoxically, in other cases, it helped to save town houses that would have been demolished or remodeled if those neighborhoods had remained fashionable. Fortunately, since World War II, an important movement has got underway in favor of preserving the old town houses in the Marais district, and it has done much to rehabilitate this eastern side of Paris. Carefully and tastefully restored, the finest of the old Marais *hôtels*—Sens, Sully, Soubise, Rohan—are now being used to house archives, museums, libraries, and cultural organizations. Open to the public, they often house exhibitions of one kind or another. But almost entirely gone are their interior decorations. The Île Saint-Louis, which declined much more gradually than the Marais, sustained less damage in this way, and it is here that one finds the purest and indeed almost the only original interiors of the mid-17th century.

The Faubourg Saint-Germain was less fortunate. During the 19th century it suffered an orgy of destruction as ministries and administrative services gradually took over this western quarter of Paris on the left bank. The offices of ministers and their departmental chiefs still have their paneling, but in all other offices the walls were systematically stripped by order of the authorities, who seem to have decided that such decorations, with their nostalgic evocation of the *ancien régime*, were incompatible with the serious business of a modern bureaucracy. Sold off for the mere price of the wood, as in the town house of Mademoiselle Desmares, or (as we know from Alfred de Champeaux) fed into the stove of the guardroom of the Army Geographical Service housed in the Hôtel de Noirmoutier, this fine wainscoting disappeared in vast quantities before 1914.

Today the Commission of Historic Monuments does its utmost to protect and preserve the interior décor of historic town houses in Paris, trying to make up for the long period when post-Renaissance embellishments were considered frivolous and expendable. But it is late in the day. To cite only one example, the entire Place Vendôme is now only an empty shell, the buildings behind the elegant façades having been taken over by the Hôtel Ritz and a number of big companies that have completely remodeled them.

Much of the life has gone out of these superb Parisian mansions. The entrances and courtyards no longer pulsate with the fine turnouts and numerous train of liveried servants such as Marcel Proust describes in his account of a reception at the home of Madame de Saint-Euverte, and such as still bustled around the Palais Rose just before World War I during the tenure there of the munificent Boni de Castellane. Those days are over. To be occupied by an embassy is one of the best fates that can befall a large Paris town house today, for then it may continue to enjoy something of that life of display and ostentation for which a long suite of drawing rooms provide the finest possible setting. And happily many of the mansions in the Faubourg Saint-Germain and the Faubourg Saint-Honoré now house foreign embassies.

With a few exceptions, the finest town houses that have remained in private hands are now divided into apartments. It is to be hoped that their tenants, respecting the interiors that provided the setting for a brilliant period of French society, can bring them to life again. After all, harmonious surroundings embellished with fine furniture and objects of quality represent one of the highest expressions of the art of living and provide a daily feast for eyes and mind.

JACQUES WILHELM
Honorary Chief Curator, Musée Carnavalet, Paris

Contents

The Marais and the île Saint-Louis

Hôtel de Sens
Hôtel de Rohan
Hôtel Sully
Hôtel de Soubise
Hôtel Carnavalet
The Arsenal
Hôtel des Ambassadeurs de Hollande
Hôtel Lauzun
Hôtel Lambert

At the Hôtel Lambert, a detail of
Le Brun's great illusionistic ceiling
for the Galerie d'Hercule

Marguerite de Valois, *la Reine Margot* (1553–1615)

Hôtel de Sens

opposite: Built between 1475 and 1507, the Hôtel de Sens is the only remaining example of a Parisian residence of the medieval period. Characteristic of Late Gothic architecture are the corners "defended" by pepper-pot turrets; also the mullioned windows and the pointed-arch portals, a large one for carriages and a smaller one for pedestrians. Originally, the tympana under the arches were filled with sculptural reliefs, as were the compartments of the turret walls. The richness of the sculptural program can be imagined from the Flamboyant Gothic finials and crockets that extend the building's vertical proportions. These elaborate, lacelike, upward thrusts seem symbolic of an age whose aspirations were Heaven-directed more than at any time since.

As a rare survivor from the Middle Ages, the Hôtel de Sens is one of the most historic houses in Paris. And it is the single edifice reproduced here that may be said truly to evoke the medieval period, for embodied within the structure are most of the picturesque features characteristic of Late Gothic secular architecture: vertical proportioning; irregular, even asymmetrical organization; thick walls penetrated by rectangular, mullioned windows and pointed-arch portals; corners defended by pepperpot turrets; high, pitched roofs; and dormers all but "aflame" with decorative stonework finials and crockets. If no other important town house has come down from medieval Paris, it is because the French, once they had gone to Italy in the late 15th-century, adopted the Renaissance with a passion, gradually replacing their secular structures with an architecture that in many respects is the anthithesis of the native Gothic.

The post-Renaissance obsession with everything medieval is a product of the Romantic era, which emerged in the mid-18th century and became dominant throughout much of the 19th century. In reaction against the Age of Reason, the Romantics looked back to the Age of Faith and sought to combat the materialistic present with nostalgia for a past when the capacity for spiritual life assured humankind of a superior place in the order of things. And the Hôtel de Sens figured large in the Gothic Revival, for it appeared in that key work of Romantic fiction, Victor Hugo's *Notre-Dame de Paris,* published in 1831. Millions were to revel in the pageant Hugo invented of the Paris of 1482. The lovely gypsy Esmeralda was waiting for them, as was the hunchback Quasimodo, the evil archdeacon Friollo, and the poet Pierre Gringoire, who found the deep, ogive portals of the Hôtel de Sens the best place to huddle for warmth on winter days.

The Hôtel de Sens was built between 1475 and 1507 for Tristan de Salazar, Archbishop of Sens. The son of a Spanish captain in French service, Tristan was a luxury-loving churchman who maintained in his town house a tapestry workshop that may have produced the superb hanging of this period that is still to be seen in Sens Cathedral. Although a cleric, he did not shrink from taking up arms and fought alongside Louis XII in the siege of Genoa, plying a lance to good effect. "He was no more worthy of being Archbishop than a Turk of being Pope," commented one unfriendly observer.

The Hôtel de Sens was also the scene when, in the late 16th century, Archbishop Renaud de Beaune heard Henri de Navarre abjure his Protestant faith—saying "Paris is worth a Mass"—in order to become Henri IV, the first of the Bourbon kings of France. Then when Henri put aside his first wife—Marguerite de Valois, the barren daughter of Henri II and Catherine de' Medici—the Archbishop let his Paris residence to the discarded Queen, popularly known as *la Reine Margot.* This marriage—like the second one that Henri IV made to Marie de' Medici—had been arranged less for love than for dynastic reasons, with the consequence that both the King and Margot had been wholly libertine in their independent search for personal solace. Indeed, Margot's licentious behavior had helped earn her an eighteen-year exile at the Château d'Usson in the Auvergne. And unhappiness followed her even to the Hôtel de Sens, for, following a brief stay there, one of her lovers, the twenty-year-old Comte de Vermond, was so indiscreet as to murder a rival, the carpenter's son Julien Date. For this crime Vermond suffered decapitation in the square below the Hôtel de Sens. Watching from a window, the distraught Margot howled: "Kill him, kill him! Here, take my garters and strangle the wretch with them." Soon, however, the memory of the murder and the execution became too much, and Queen Margot moved to another house near the abbey at Saint-Germain-des-Prés.

From 1650 until the French Revolution, the Sens prelates continuously let their Paris hôtel to tenants. For much of this period the house served as a terminal for the mail coaches and other carriages connecting Paris to Lyons, Burgundy, and the Franche-Comté. Confiscated in the upheaval of 1789–94, the noble residence was savagely taken over by commercial interests and divided into apartments. In 1841–43, one of these sheltered Alexandre Schanne, the model for Schaunard in Murger's novel *La Vie de bohème,* which achieved fame as the book upon which Puccini based his opera *La Bohème.*

The city of Paris acquired the Hôtel de Sens in 1911 and proceeded to restore and even to rebuild it. The structure is now the home of the Bibliothèque Forney, a library documenting the arts and crafts of France, England, and Holland.

The courtyard façade of the late 15th-century Hôtel de Sens is a modern reconstruction.

Hôtel de Rohan

There may be no better introduction to the architecture of the 18th century than the façade of the Hôtel de Rohan, erected in 1705–08 from plans by Alexandre Delamair, who was also responsible for the exterior of the adjacent Hôtel de Soubise. The Greco-Roman vocabulary of architectural forms had prevailed in France since the early 16th century, when François I brought the Renaissance from Italy and began the long process of substituting it for the native Gothic. Now the planning became regular, rational, even symmetrical, while the proportions increasingly tended away from the vertical and the "spiritual" toward the horizontal and the humanistic. Corners shed their defensive towers; windows opened large; and the styling, of course, rested upon the temple architecture of classical antiquity. In the 17th century—France's *grand siècle*—Louis XIV urged that the Renaissance mode be expanded to a scale of unprecedented grandeur, the better to symbolize a regime committed totally to the principle of monarchical absolutism. All this had been accomplished when the King died in 1715, after a reign of seventy-two years! Now the French had had enough of grandeur and preferred to cultivate a gratifying synthesis of what would appear to be the polar opposites of comfort and elegance. The façade of the Hôtel de Rohan, cool and harmonious but not too imposing, allows us to suspect the livable interiors, with their refined surfaces and intimate scale, that would be the particular contribution of the new century.

left: The garden façade of the Hôtel de Rohan, built in 1705–08 from plans by Alexandre Delamair, is a distinct triumph of French Baroque classicism at its most elegant and refined. Sobriety reigns in the structure's symmetry and centrality, which in shallow, stepwise fashion projects the central bay as a modified temple front of superimposed Doric and Ionic colonnades crowned by a low, simple pediment. But everything is lightened by the slender proportions, the exceptionally large, story-high windows, and the delicately wrought iron grilles that grace the lower part of all openings on the *étage noble.* **below:** For the courtyard stables at the Hôtel de Rohan, Robert Le Lorrain created a masterpiece in *The Horses of the Sun.* Making hard materials look as fluid as paint, the artist displayed a command of pictorial illusionism that is a true hallmark of the virtuoso 18th century.

The Hôtel de Rohan was commissioned by the scion of an ancient line whose ancestral seat remains the Château de Josselin in Brittany and whose motto says much for the family stance in the world: *Roi ne suis, duc ne daigne, Rohan suis,* or "King I cannot be, Duke I disdain, Rohan I am." Rohan pride triumphed in the builder of the new hôtel in Paris, for there were many who presumed Armand-Gaston-Maximilien de Rohan-Soubise to be the son of Louis XIV and Anne de Rohan-Chabot. The young man himself seems to have taken this for granted. Thanks to the unbridled ambition of his mother and the favor of the King, who always singled him out above the other children of Madame de Soubise, he was made Canon-Count of Strasbourg in 1694, at the age of twenty, and ten years later Prince-Bishop of Strasbourg, one of the richest sees in France. This precocious and brilliant career climaxed in 1712 when Armand-Gaston received a Cardinal's hat and once more in 1713 when he gained the office of Grand Almoner. Saint-Simon, who detested the Rohans, admitted in his memoirs that the Cardinal was "a man of parts, still further enhanced by the graces of his person, his expression, the select society in which he had been schooled, and by the love affairs and intrigues that Madame de Soubise had put him in the way of. Mild and easygoing in disposition, unambitious, and free of the compulsions that ambition imposes, he was a gentleman and a person of honor. Moreover, he was engaging and obliging, perfectly courteous in his demeanor to everyone, but with moderation and distinction." For all his prudence, however, Cardinal de Rohan-Soubise became involved in the ugly quarrels between the Jesuits and the Jansenists. The latter, who might almost have passed for Presbyterians pretending to be Roman Catholics, were a thorn in the flesh of Louis XIV and a nuisance to Pope Clement XI, who condemned the sect in the famous bull *Unigenitus* of 1713.

On the death of Cardinal de Rohan-Soubise in 1749, the bishopric of Strasbourg and the Paris town house passed to a nephew, Armand, Cardinal de Soubise, then in 1756 to the latter's cousin, Louis-Constantin de Rohan, who died in 1779. The inheritance next fell to Cardinal Louis-René-Édouard de Rohan—the sad and silly dupe in the infamous "diamond necklace affair" that so wantonly damaged the reputation of Marie-Antoinette. This Rohan was handsome, everyone admitted, but "not at all what he should have been," wrote a governess in her recollections. "Yet he was as kind as a man can be outside of his official position." In 1772 Louis de Rohan was made France's ambassador to Vienna. "In sending so frivolous and immoral a man as Prince Louis de Rohan, no worse choice could have been made, nor one more disagreeable to Maria-Theresa," declared Madame de Campan, who served as Marie-Antoinette's secretary. "He was the merest dabbler and knew nothing that could be turned to advantage in diplomacy. His reputation had preceded him, and his mission was begun under the most unfavorable auspices. Running out of money, he fell into debt for over a million and imagined that he could impress the Viennese and the court. He brought with him eight or ten gentlemen with fine names, a dozen equally well-born pages, a host of officers and footmen, not to mention a chamber music group. But this empty show could not last for long. Finding they were getting no wages, his people abused their diplomatic immunity in order to make money by smuggling. (I have often heard the Queen say that in one year more silk stockings were sold in the Prince de Rohan's office in Vienna than in all Lyons and Paris.) The situation was so shameless that to put an end to it, Maria-Theresa was obliged to abolish the privileges of the entire diplomatic corps, which made the person and conduct of Prince Louis odious in the eyes of all the foreign courts." Yet Rohan power at

above: The spacious vestibule in the Hôtel de Rohan, flooded with light from five story-high windows, leads to the ground-floor drawing rooms, all of which were given over to the superb library collected by four generations of Rohan Cardinals. **opposite:** The exquisitely Rococo paneling of the "Green Salon," located on the *étage noble* of the Hôtel de Rohan, was made originally for a small room in the adjacent Hôtel de Soubise. The carved "shellwork" enframements and medallions, depicting scenes from the *Fables* of La Fontaine, are gilded and stand in relief against a bluish-green ground that is a precious example of *vernis Martin,* a lacquer created by the Martin brothers that was the rage in 18th-century France.

home earned him the position of Grand Almoner in 1778, Cardinal in 1778, and Prince-Bishop of Strasbourg in 1779. For the sorry role he played in the necklace fraud, Cardinal Louis was arrested on August 15, 1785, just as he was robed and ready to celebrate Mass in the chapel at Versailles. Exiled to La Chaise-Dieu, then sent to the Estates-General in 1789 as a representative of the nobility, he soon emigrated to Ettenheim in Württenberg, a German section of his diocese, where he died at age sixty-nine in 1803.

Confiscated during the Revolution, the Hôtel de Rohan was emptied of its furniture. However, the magnificent library collected by the Rohan Cardinals, having been purchased in 1789 by the Comte d'Artois, Louis XVI's younger brother, was saved and transferred to the Arsenal. In recent years the great house has been intelligently restored and special care taken of the Cabinet des Singes, famous for the wall panels painted in a deliciously Rococo manner by Christophe Huet.

above: The Hôtel de Rohan has lost most of the paneling that once decorated its main suites, with the fortunate exception of the Cabinet des Singes, or "Monkey Room." There, in designs painted about 1750 by Christophe Huet, monkeys frolic among the tendrils of the arabesque enframements, which contain pastoral scenes of exotically attired young folk occupied in such games as leap frog and blind man's buff. The panels on the left conceal a passage to a small oratory, which, oddly enough, was as close as this house of prelates came to having a chapel.   **opposite:** The dining room, as well as the anteroom, is hung with tapestries whose *chinoiserie* themes were taken from paintings by François Boucher. The woodwork surrounding them is modern.

Louis, Cardinal de Rohan (1734–1803)

Maximilien de Béthune, Duc de Sully (1559–1641)

Hôtel Sully

The Hôtel Sully is a key monument in Paris disclosing the state of French classicism as it had developed in the early part of the nation's *grand siècle*, somewhat over a century after the Italian Renaissance had been introduced into France. The building, which dates from 1624–30, was erected from designs prepared by Jean-Androuet Du Cerceau, better known for his horseshoe staircase at Fontainebleau. This was the age of Louis XIII and of Cardinal Richelieu, the King's all-powerful first minister, and a time when so many of the institutions that would shape modern France—including the Academy—were being established. The four-square regularity of the planning and the Greco-Roman detailing show that the French had learned much about the revived Mediterranean tradition. Still, the steep roofs, the high dormers, and the overall verticality, as well as the niched figural reliefs in the manner of Jean Goujon, a major master of the preceding century, indicate that in the Hôtel Sully—magnificent as it is—French designers remained somewhat tentative in their development toward the idiomatic classicism that soon would dominate European architecture, and do so continuously, for almost two centuries.

The mansion was put up for Mesme-Gallet, the lord of Le Petit-Thouard and of La Jaille who in Paris held the office of comptroller of the mint. A compulsive gambler, Mesme-Gallet found himself ruined with debt and sold the building even before it was completed. Subsequently, in 1634, after belonging to two other parties, the hôtel was bought by Maximilien de Béthune, Baron de Rosny and Duc de Sully,

The Late Renaissance–Early Baroque façade in the courtyard of the Hôtel Sully, erected between 1621 and 1630 from plans thought to be by Jean-Androuet Du Cerceau.

below: This small salon in the Hôtel Sully has recently been hung with a set of tapestries that, in view of their perfect fit and their previous location in the Château de Sully-sur-Loire, may well have been originally designed for their present location. **right:** The bedroom of the second Duchesse de Sully was sumptuously redone in 1660 in the manner of classical architecture, complete with Corinthian pilasters, a richly carved cornice, and pediments supported on scrolls. The bed and its hanging are modern reconstructions from period designs.

who had been the statesman most responsible for bringing glory to the reign of Henri IV. Thus, almost a quarter-century after the assassination of *le bon roi* Henri, the great Sully moved into the hôtel that ever since has borne his name.

It was at the Hôtel Sully, that, in 1726, the young Voltaire ran into the trouble that would result in his incarceration and subsequent exile in England. The affair had actually commenced several days earlier at the Comédie-Française, in the loge of the celebrated actress Adrienne Lecouvreur. Jealous of the presence there of the witty, engaging Voltaire, the Chevalier de Rohan-Chabot, a nephew of the Princesse de Soubise, determined to be insolent: "What is your name? Arouet? Voltaire? In fact, have you a name?" Characteristically, Voltaire retorted: "I am just making my name, while you are finishing yours!" To save Voltaire from being struck by an aristocratic cane, Mademoiselle Lecouvreur oppor-

opposite: In 1660 the ceiling over the bedroom of the second Duchesse de Sully was painted with an illusionistic scene depicting "The Abduction of Endymion." The artist—the little-known Antoine Paillet—then filled the spandrels with *trompe l'oeil* plaster reliefs symbolizing the four times of day.   **right:** At the bottom of the Hôtel Sully's garden stands another building, known as the "Petit Sully," the public façade of which is oriented toward the Place des Vosges. Originally the ground floor of this structure served as an *orangerie*.

tunely staged a fainting spell. Shortly thereafter, while dining at the Hôtel Sully, Voltaire received word that a messenger was awaiting him in the street below. Arriving there, he was suddenly seized and beaten by a trio of men all the while that Rohan-Chabot watched from his carriage. The assault continued until finally the Chevalier announced: "Enough! Don't hit him on the head; something good may come out of it in the end!" Even Voltaire's host, the Duc de Sully, was not particularly disturbed that a Rohan should take it upon himself to chastise a man of letters. When Voltaire announced that he would challenge his adversary to a duel, the latter obtained a *lettre de cachet* from Louis XV, which sent the poet to the Bastille.

After 1752 the Hôtel Sully belonged to Turgot de Saint-Clair, a counselor to the Parlement of Paris, and then to his daughter, the Comtesse de Boisgelin. Beginning in 1796, the mansion was divided into apartments; it suffered further damage throughout the 19th century. Recently restored, the hôtel now houses France's Historic Monuments Commission.

Charles de Rohan, Marshal of France and Prince de Soubise (1715–87)

Hôtel de Soubise

"Masterpiece" seems rather too stale a word to describe the Salon de la Princesse (1736–39), that ever-fresh glory of the Hôtel de Soubise conceived by Germain Boffrand for the second Prince de Soubise, Duc de Rohan-Rohan. Here is the immortal symbol of the Rococo, whose curvilinear caprices have never failed to enchant the most sophisticated connoisseurs of the 18th century. This oval, light-filled drawing room may be compared to only one other marvel of the Rococo style, the interior of the Amalienburg pavilion in Munich's Nymphenburg gardens. But the Amalienburg was contrived a year or two later by François de Cuvilliès, the court dwarf who, as a Frenchman, knew the latest developments in Paris and became architect to the Elector of Bavaria. Boffrand had been one of the most imaginative pupils of Jules Hardouin-Mansart, Louis XIV's favorite architect. Thus, long before the triumph at the Hôtel de Soubise, Boffrand had demonstrated something of his genius for decorative eloquence at the Château de Lunéville, the seat of Léopold, Duc de Lorraine. Also in the Lorraine, he had created the Château de Craon at Haroué, this time working for the Duke's mistress. No less popular in Paris, Boffrand planned both the Hôtel de Seignelay and the Hôtel de Beauharnais, in addition to the Hôtel de Soubise.

A paradigm of French 18th-century classicism, the façade of the Hôtel de Soubise was built in 1705–09 from designs by Delamair, whose assignment was to modernize the former Hôtel de Guise. For the *cour d'honneur*, Delamair transformed the old Guise *manège*—an oval area used for exercising horses—into a beautiful peristyle of fifty-six paired columns. Atop the façade's pediment rest two sculptural groups representing the Four Seasons and two reclining personifications of Glory and Magnificence. All are the work of Robert Le Lorrain.

The architect responsible for the actual structure of the Hôtel de Soubise (1705–09) was Alexandre Delamair, who lost his mind after designing this mansion and the adjacent Hôtel de Rohan. The Soubise project, with its noble yet engaging façade, was one that came about as a consequence of a particularly strong fancy that Louis XIV had taken for the second wife of François de Rohan, Prince de Soubise. A ravishing redhead, the former Anne de Rohan-Chabot, now Princesse de Soubise, had become lady-in-waiting to the Queen in the days when the King was devoted to Madame de Montespan. But, once she was at court, wrote the Duc de Saint-Simon, "her beauty did the rest. In no time the King fell in love with her. Everything has its season, and Madame de Montespan was beginning to bore him."

The site occupied by the Hôtel de Soubise was already an historic one, long associated with the aristocracy. Evidence of this lingers on the Rue des Archives, where the side entrance to the Hôtel de Soubise is, incongruously, a Gothic portal fortified by a pair of pepper-pot turrets.

below: At the Hôtel de Soubise, the sole vestige still visible of the house erected in 1371–75 for Olivier de Clisson, the immensely wealthy constable of France, is a gatehouse fortified by a pair of pepper-pot turrets. This incongruity was left standing when the Hôtel de Soubise underwent remodeling in the early 18th century and again in the 19th century. **right:** Originally, façades of the Soubise mansion and the Hôtel de Rohan were oriented toward one another across a large enclosed garden, as can be seen in a detail from Turgot's old plan of Paris. During the 19th century, new structures were put up in the garden, thus separating the two great hôtels of the Rohan family.

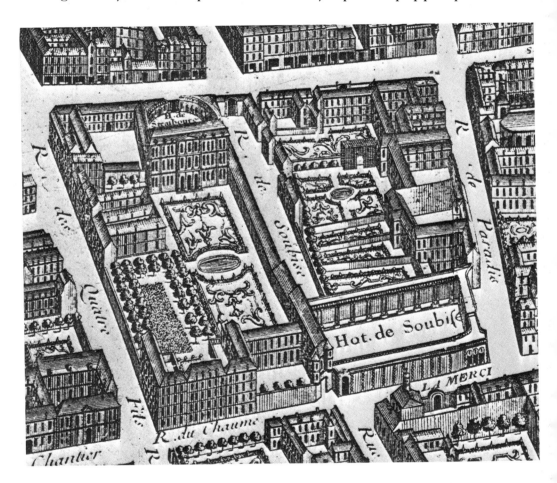

opposite: On the ground floor of the Hôtel de Soubise, in what was a pavilion at the center of the garden façade, is the salon decorated by Germain Boffrand in 1735–36 for Prince Hercule-Mériadec de Soubise. Thanks to a recent restoration, the magnificient décor has regained its original colors—white and flax blue—with gilding reserved for the richly carved mirror frames. Also carefully restored are the stucco reliefs in the spandrels, creations of L. S. Adam and J. B. Lemoyne.

This feudal vestige survives from the house erected in 1371–75 by Olivier de Clisson, constable of France during a critical period of the Hundred Years War and one of the wealthiest men of his time. By the middle of the 16th century, the mansion had been acquired by the Guises, that all-powerful Catholic family in the days when the forces of Reformation threatened the unity and stability of France. Under these lords the hôtel was considerably enlarged and sumptuously decorated by Primaticcio, one of the most important of the Italian masters who formed the School of Fontainebleau and through it brought the Renaissance to France. But the most celebrated of the paintings were those done in the chapel by Nicolà dell'Abate. Now a true palace, the Hôtel de Guise became the scene of splendid *fêtes,* among the more memorable of which were those staged on the occasion of the marriage of the Princesse Claude, daughter of Henri II and Catherine de' Medici. It was also at the Hôtel de Guise, during the reign there of Duke Henri, popularly known

Henri de Lorraine (1550–88), the Duc de Guise *(Le Balafré)* whose power so threatened the throne that Henri III had him slain in the royal apartments at Blois.

Anne d'Este (d. 1607), the granddaughter of Louis XII who married François de Lorraine, Duc de Guise, and in 1553 acquired the hôtel that became the Paris residence of the powerful Guise family.

as *Le Balafré* ("Scarface"), that the first discussions got under way leading to the Saint Bartholomew's Day Massacre on August 24, 1572, which rid France of its chief Huguenots while these were gathered in Paris for the wedding of Marguerite de Valois (the sister of Claude) to Henri de Navarre, the future Henri IV of France. Thereafter the Duc de Guise, as head of the League, gained such ascendancy that even the King, Henri III, feared him. While the Guise family controlled the Parisian mob, which was ever ready to mount the barricades in support of the Catholic cause, Catherine de' Medici repeatedly called at the Hôtel de Guise in the hope of assuaging its masters' wrath, which now was fueled by aid from Philip II of Spain. Finally, by 1588, the power held by the Guise faction was too great to be tolerated, and while the court was gathered at Blois Le Balafré and his brother, the Cardinal de Lorraine, fell under assassins' knives. It proved to be a grisly occasion, with the King watching in mock disbelief as the Duc de Guise staggered, bleeding, from room to room in the royal suite.

The last Duc de Guise was the 17th-century grandee who arranged the famous *fêtes* and carrousels that inaugurated the reign of Louis XIV. During his tenure the Hôtel de Guise sheltered a variety of men of letters, among them Tristan L'Hermite and, in his late years, the great playwright Pierre Corneille. Surviving the Duke was his sister, Mademoiselle de Guise, whose own death in 1688 extinguished the line. The nearest relatives were the Princesse de Condé and the Duchesse de Hanovre, who sold the Hôtel de Guise to the Prince de Soubise in 1705.

In rebuilding the old palace, Prince François de Soubise followed the advice of his son, the Bishop of Strasbourg whose real father was presumed to have been Louis XIV, and engaged Delamair to draw up the plans. The King continued to favor the Soubise family even after its original attraction for him—Anne de Rohan-Chabot—had died. In 1714 he changed the domain of Frontenay into the duchy of Rohan-Rohan for the benefit of the Soubises' eldest son, Hercule-Mériadec.

When this Soubise remarried in 1732, at age sixty-three, he took as wife the nineteen-year-old Marie-Sophie de Courcillon, the Princess for whom Boffrand, in 1732–40, created the superb rooms in the Hôtel de Soubise that established the Rococo style and with it seduced the whole of Europe.

The next Prince de Soubise, Charles de Rohan, who succeeded to the title in 1749, proved immensely popular at the court of Louis XV and managed to gain the patronage of both Madame de Pompadour and her successor, Madame du Barry. The former even arranged, over the objections of much of the royal house, a marriage between Prince Charles' daughter and the Prince de Condé, a direct descendant in a collateral line of the Bourbon family. She also succeeded in making him an army commander during the Seven Years War, a favor that turned sour, however, when Soubise lost the Battle of Rossbach in 1757. Then in 1758 at Lutzelberg he had a victory and with it came the baton of a marshal of France. A year later he was made minister of state. Meanwhile, Soubise and his third wife, Anne-Victoire de Hesse-Rheinfels, regaled fashionable Paris with their respective infidelities, the Princess in an elopement with the Soubise jewels and the Prince with a string of dancers from the opera. Still, at the end of Louis XV's reign Prince Charles had the grace to prove the monarch wrong in his famous complaint: "Whenever I grant a favor, I make twenty malcontents and one ingrate." It was a very grateful Prince de Soubise who, alone, accompanied the dead King's remains the full distance to their resting place in at Saint-Denis.

Prince Charles was also perfectly charming, according to the Duc de Croÿ, who described the fabulous occasion that Soubise made of the re-

Anne de Rohan-Chabot, Princesse de Soubise (d. before 1715), whose high-colored beauty brought attention from Louis XIV and the great wealth that made possible the Hôtel de Soubise.

opening of the family hôtel some six years before Rossbach: "It is said that, outside the court, nothing so splendid has been seen for twenty years. . . . Room after room and the full extent of the great staircase, that superb house was ablaze with lights. A host of the very best people, the service, and the magnificence of everything reflected the greatest credit on the Prince." But Prince Charles won even greater fame as a patron of the arts, especially in the concerts arranged at the Hôtel de Soubise, and in the astonishing town house he commissioned—from the great Claude-Nicolas Ledoux—for the benefit of the dancer Mademoiselle Guimard. This brilliant invention has vanished, but Thomas Jefferson, who chanced to see it, memorized the façade and echoed its austere grace in Pavilion IX of the University of Virginia at Charlottesville.

In his old age Prince Charles was troubled, first, by the spectacular bankruptcy of his son-in-law and nephew, the Prince de Guémenée and, then, by the involvement of his kinsman, the unforgivably stupid and irresponsible Cardinal Louis de Rohan, in the notorious "diamond necklace affair," which brought undeserved dishonor to Marie-Antoinette. Prince Charles died in 1787, two years before the fall of the Bastille, in a relatively modest house on the Rue de l'Arcade, the Hôtel de Soubise being by then beyond his means.

After the Revolution, the Princesse de Guémenée, who had been the official governess of the children of Louis XVI and Marie-Antoinette— that is, until the embarrassment of her husband's bankruptcy—recovered her father's house, only to have creditors sell it to a speculator. In 1808 the French state acquired the mansion and made it the home of the National Archives. The building was much altered in the 19th century, its grand staircase reconstructed, the private apartments demolished, and new structures put up in the garden, separating the Hôtel de Soubise from its adjacent neighbor, the Hôtel de Rohan. Preserved and recently restored, however, were those timeless masterpieces—the *cour d'honneur* and the apartments created by Boffrand for Prince Hercule and Princess Marie.

In the Hôtel de Soubise the state bedroom **(above)** and the salon **(right)** of Marie-Sophie de Courcillon, Princesse de Soubise, are the key and founding masterpieces of the entire Rococo style. Created by Germain Boffrand in 1736–37, the design of the salon corresponds to that made for the Prince's drawing room, except that here all the relief work is gilded, while the spandrels are filled, not with stucco sculpture, but with full-color paintings by Natoire, who took as his theme the story of Psyche. In the bedroom the fabrics are 19th-century reconstructions.

Madame de Sévigné (1626–96)

Hôtel Carnavalet

above: At the Hôtel Carnavalet, architecturally important fragments from Parisian buildings destroyed in the 19th century have been reconstructed in the garden. Among the most significant vestiges are the forward sections—a central monumental gate and lateral loggias—saved from the Hôtel de Choiseul, an early 18th-century structure that stood in the Rue Saint-Augustin. **opposite:** This charming room was created about 1650 for the Hôtel Colbert de Villacerf, which still exists at 23 Rue de Turenne. The decorative themes are opulently Roman, with some of the paintings done in flat, arabesque patterns, while others, especially on the coved ceiling sections, are illusionistic.

A fine and historic house in the Marais, the Hôtel Carnavalet has an even greater claim to fame by virtue of the long residence there of one of the true adornments of French civilization—Marie de Rabutin-Chantal, Marquise de Sévigné (1626–96). Madame de Sévigné may not be the favorite author of every grandparent, but she ranked very high in the esteem of Marcel Proust's grandmother, and connoisseurs of the art of letter-writing have never found anything to surpass the correspondence that simply flooded from the pen of the sharp-eyed, principled, ever-witty, and articulate Marquise. In the world of eloquent discourse nothing quite equals the charm and accuracy of the accounts she sent her daughter, the Comtesse de Grignan, of life at the court of Louis XIV. Altogether, the more than fifteen hundred epistles collected from the correspondence of Madame de Sévigné constitute an invaluable and ingratiating chronicle of France's *grand siècle* at its zenith. The Marquise worshiped Fouquet, the finance minister the King dismissed and then jailed after inspecting the glories of his estate, Vaux-le-Vicomte, and Fouquet lives on in her pages. So does the legendary Vatel, Fouquet's chef. Later, in the service of the Prince de Condé at Chantilly, Vatel killed himself when he discovered, to his horror, that the fish had failed to arrive in time for a banquet Condé was offering to His Majesty. Finally, we learn from Madame de Sévigné that ecstasy was out of place in the Royal Presence. She was speechless, she told the King, on witnessing a performance of the great Racine's *Esther*. "The man is clever," decided Louis XIV.

Now a museum dedicated to the history of Paris and of French furniture and decorative arts, the Carnavalet first assumed importance when Madame de Sévigné settled there in October 1677. "Thank God, we have the Hôtel Carnavalet," she reported shortly after moving day. "And since we can't have everything, we must get along without parquet floors and the little fireplaces that are so fashionable nowadays, but at least we'll have a handsome courtyard and a beautiful garden, all in a fine part of town. Besides, there are those pretty girls in blue next door." Here the Marquise referred to the neighboring convent of the Anonciales.

At the Hôtel Carnavalet, Madame de Sévigné made her home in a suite of rooms on the *premier étage* (the second story), while reserving the ground floor for her daughter and son-in-law, the governor of Provence, whenever they were in town. The wings and the building on the street were occupied by the Marquise's son and by the Abbé de Coulanges, whom the châtelaine baptized *le bien Bon*. In her *carnavalette* the Marquise presided over one of Paris' most fashionable salons, loyally frequented by the Duc de La Rochefoucauld, the author of wry maxims that still seem fresh, and by Madame de La Fayette, whose *Princesse de Clèves* is surely the greatest of the early French novels. Also in attendance were Cardinal de Retz, Chancellor Séguier, and Bossuet, the great orator-Bishop of Meaux. How close Madame de Sévigné was to her mischievous cousin Comte Roger de Bussy-Rabutin is a question. Another of the period's great letter-writers and chroniclers, Comte Roger was also a notorious scandal monger whose caprices in this regard earned him stays in the Bastille and exile to his estate in Burgundy. Even so, he gained a chair at the French Academy, in recognition of his more serious work. The Marquise, who could take anyone down, liked nothing better than putting her cousin in his place. On one occasion he bothered to inform her of the Marquis de Sévigné's affair with the famous courtesan Ninon de Lenclos, only to be told: "I'm not half so angry as you would like to believe."

The Hôtel Carnavalet was built at the height of the French Renaissance—about 1548–60—for Jacques de Ligneris, the judge sent by François I to represent France at the Council of Trent, which launched the Catholic Counter-Reformation. In 1578 Ligneris' heir sold the house to the widow of François de Kernevenoy, who, known as Carnavalet, gave the mansion its name. Once the tutor to the Duc d'Anjou, the future Henri III, this owner is also remembered for his horsemanship, which Montaigne saluted as did Ronsard:

> *Dirai-je l'expérience*
> *Que tu as en la science*
> *Ou ta main qui sait l'adresse*
> *De façonner la jeunesse*
> *L'acheminant à bon train,*
> *Ou ton art qui admoneste*
> *L'esprit de la fière beste*
> *Se rendre docile au frein.*

Six years before her death in 1608 Madame de Kernevenoy sold the house to Florent d'Argouges, treasurer to Marie de' Medici, Henri IV's Queen. After 1654 the rich army contractor Claude Boislève owned the property and had it enlarged by François Mansart, who raised the height of the wings and street front. Hardly had this remodeling been accomplished when Boislève was engulfed by the storm raging about Fouquet. This brought the Carnavalet a new owner, Monsieur d'Agaury, who was happy to lease the mansion to Madame de Sévigné.

left: At the Hôtel Carnavalet the façade at the bottom of the courtyard has remained very much as it was constructed in 1548–60 by Nicolas Dupuis. Only the balustrade and dormers are 19th-century reconstructions. The superb relief carvings on the upper wall, which depict personifications of the Four Seasons accompanied by appropriate signs of the zodiac **(below)**, are attributed to the atelier of Jean Goujon, the greatest sculptor of the French Renaissance.

At the Hôtel Carnavalet the gallery **(right)** and the salon that it leads to **(below)** retain the decorations installed there around 1700, shortly after Madame de Sévigné died in 1696. The arms of her family now found over the salon windows are 19th-century additions. The gallery, with its fine but simple paneling, contains a portrait of the famous letter-writer, a desk bearing her arms, and a portrait of her daughter, the Comtesse de Grignan. The salon is furnished with a small Régence table, finished in imitation blue and white faience, and a pair of superb Louis XV *fauteuils,* all part of the Bouvier bequest.

After the Marquise's death in 1696, the Hôtel de Carnavalet changed hands again and again. Sold and stripped during the Revolution, it became the headquarters of the government printing office under the Empire. From 1814 to 1829 the building was occupied by the School of Civil Engineering. Only after 1866 did the great house become the museum it remains. This was made possible by the city of Paris, which purchased the Carnavalet, restored and enlarged it, and then began adding, especially in the gardens, valuable fragments from other buildings, such as the old Palais de Justice, the Drapers' Hall erected by Jacques Bruant in 1655, and the Hôtel de Choiseul. Meanwhile, the interiors have been installed with paneling salvaged from fine old hôtels destroyed in the 19th century. Recently the Bouvier bequest has added an important collection to the Carnavalet's already superb holdings in furnishings and the decorative arts. Of particular importance are the relief sculptures of the Four Seasons that remain on the courtyard façade from the time of the Carnavalet's original construction in the 16th century. These beautiful works are attributed to the workshop of Jean Goujon.

The Carnavalet shelters some rare and prize decorations created by Claude-Nicolas Ledoux, France's greatest architect in the second half of the 18th century and the chief author of the aesthetic reform that led away from the complex, curvilinear graces of the Rococo and toward the monumental simplicities of the Neoclassical style. The paneling from the Café Militaire in the Palais-Royal **(above)** is the first known work by Ledoux. Executed in 1762, the interior met with instant success, as we know from an article written by the critic Élie Fréron and published in *L'Année littéraire*. The plain rectangular panels, emblazoned with trophies and flanked by pilasters in the form of lictors' fasces supporting plumed helmets gave a whole new meaning to elegance in an age that specialized in this quality. The success of the Café Militaire decorations brought Ledoux the important commission for the Hôtel d'Uzès. Built in 1767, this masterpiece was destroyed during the Second Empire. But the Carnavalet has recently acquired the surviving woodwork from the main salon **(opposite)**. Highly original, the large panels display tall, slender "trees" sprouting not only leaves but also shields, helmets, weapons, and musical instruments. The effect is stylish but also rather intellectual and abstract.

below: At the Carnavalet the complete surround of charmingly idyllic landscape scenes, rich in both flora and fauna, was painted about 1765 for the engraver Demarteau by François Boucher and his atelier, assisted by Jean-Honoré Fragonard and that great *animalier,* Jean-Baptiste Huet. The Rococo paneling of the Blue Room **(right above)** originated in the Hôtel Brulart de Genlis on the Quai Conti, while that in the Yellow Room was made for the Hôtel d'Aubigny in the Rue Malebranche. These rooms all form part of the rich Bouvier bequest.

The Arsenal in the 18th century.

The Arsenal

An arsenal might well be the last place on earth where one would look for either a mischievous Duchess with the stature of a dwarf, or rare *boiseries* realized in the most beautiful Rococo manner, or indeed a Romantic writer doubling as a librarian, a writer as well acquainted with vampires as with the literary celebrities of his era. Yet all three phenomena were to be encountered at the Paris Arsenal, mainly because of a long tradition that made the titular director of this institution a person of rather considerable social and cultural standing. The appointment gave him and his family a fine and spacious town residence; better yet, it provided the leisure in which to live well and think long. Thus, in a way uniquely French, the Paris Arsenal has an almost unbroken history, from the time of Louis XIV on, of vigorous salon life, which brought to the cannon factory not only a good portion of the world of letters, but also the kind of bibliophile spirit that has made this great house the repository of the richest library now to be found in France outside the Bibliothèque Nationale itself.

The story of the Arsenal begins in 1512, when the city of Paris, on orders from Louis XI, erected in a southeastern sector of the capital, between the Bastille and the Seine, a *grange* ("barn") for the founding of cannon. Twenty years later François I enlarged the foundry, mainly by purchasing land from the adjacent convent of the Célestins, and transformed the establishment into the Royal Arsenal. Gun powder was put into manufacture at the Arsenal, and the whole thing blew up in 1562. Charles IX thereupon commissioned a set of new buildings, to be erected from plans by Philibert Delorme, the greatest architect of the French Renaissance. Now the Arsenal gained a *logis* for a director bearing the title of Grand Master of the Artillery. The first to occupy the new position and hôtel was Armand de Gontaut-Biron.

The Arsenal post next went to none other than Maximilien de

above: The poet Charles Nodier was librarian at the Arsenal from 1824 to 1844, there maintaining a literary salon that became the center of France's Romantic movement. **left:** The room that Charles Nodier used for dining has retained its fine 17th-century paneling, carved with trophies that provide a grandiose enframement for a flower painting executed in the manner of Monnoyer.

Béthune, the great minister who as Duc de Sully did so much to make the reign of Henri IV a time of national reconsolidation leading to France's *grand siècle*. While in office, Sully lived at the Arsenal (buying what would become the Hôtel Sully only after his retirement). There he often received the King, who so liked the environment that he was even planning to make a place for himself—until assassination abruptly ended *le bon roi* Henri's reign in 1610.

Under the next regime, that of Louis XIII, Richelieu succeeded Sully as chief minister, but not in his position at the Arsenal. Instead, the Cardinal made the Arsenal the seat of a court of justice for special crimes, which in 1664 would try Fouquet, when this great superintendent of finances had his sensational fall from power under Louis XIV. In 1680 it would also try the odious poisoner called La Voisin, quickly condemning her to burn alive when the evidence began to implicate some of the more prominent members of the court. Meanwhile, Louis XIV transferred the manufacture of cannon to the Salpetrière, leaving the Arsenal foundry

Alfred de Vigny (1797–1863)

The salon of Charles Nodier at the Arsenal in the second quarter of the 19th century

Marie Nodier (1811–83),
the poet's daughter

to the Keller *frères,* who cast much of the huge sculptural population destined for the gardens at Versailles.

In the France of *le roi soleil* this made the Arsenal a particularly important place; thus, in 1694 the King filled the position of Grand Master of the Artillery with his own favorite son, the Duc du Maine, born of a royal affair with La Montespan, but now legitimatized. The young director initiated a vast new building program, which created the Arsenal we now know. The architect in charge was Germain Boffrand, whose ideas can be found in the façade that, with its drastic 19th-century revisions, fronts on the Boulevard Morland.

The Duc du Maine was a shy person with literary tastes and a scholarly bent that made translating from the Latin his favorite diversion. Marriage allied him to the famously diminutive but monumentally ambitious daughter of *le grand* Condé, a prince of the blood and the greatest of France's 17th-century generals. She too favored the world of letters and cultivated a literary salon—at the châteaux of Anet and Sceaux as well as at the Arsenal—in which the brightest lights were Voltaire and Madame du Châtelet. Unfortunately, the Duchesse du Maine also liked to dabble in dynastic plotting, a propensity that sent both her and her husband to the Bastille for a time.

In the aftermath of the Duc du Maine's tenure the title of the Arsenal director was reduced to Bailiff of the French Artillery. The first person to receive it was Antoine-René de Boyer d'Argenson, Marquis de Paulmy, whose passion for books gave the Arsenal its first reputation as a library. The importance of the Paulmy volumes attracted the Comte d'Artois, Louis XVI's cultivated younger brother, who after buying the collection in 1785, and saving it from destruction during the Revolution, returned it to the Arsenal upon his abdication as Charles X in 1830. In the interim, under the Empire, the Arsenal was officially transformed into a library. Madame de Genlis lived there for some years, maintaining Napoleonic Paris' most important salon, avidly attended by such literati as Millevoye, La Harpe, Fontanes, and Chateaubriand, as well as by the politicians Talleyrand, Bernadotte, and Caulaincourt. From the Arsenal she sent the Emperor a monthly *lettre d'information* designed to keep him apprised of current opinion. Throughout the 19th century the Arsenal had one distinguished director after another: Saint-Simon, the former aristocrat who aided the American Revolution and returned to France to found a cult of Christian socialism; Charles Nodier, the poet of "vampires" whose circle at the Arsenal (Victor Hugo, Alfred de Vigny, Alfred de Musset, etc.) formed the nucleus of the whole Romantic movement; José Maria de Heredia, a leading member of the Parnassian group of poets; and finally Maurice Barrès, the French nationalist whose trilogy of novels *Le culte du moi* (1888–91) advocated a kind of ego worship that anticipated the Freudian, Surrealist 20th century.

Alfred de Musset (1810–57)

Much of the legendary liveliness of the Nodier era may have come from the spirit of generosity encouraged by the host toward all who made a creative effort, which also led to some absurdities as well as to new heights of wit. "The most laudatory epithets," recorded Madame Ancelot, "were lavished upon the feeblest, the worst, or even the most ridiculous things, with the result that the usual terms of praise were no longer possible for the performances of the truly fine talents who regularly came to the Nodiers'. Thus, it was decided to play God and invent a kind of secret language that would be spoken only by the initiates. . . . For instance, when Hugo . . . recited in that powerful, monotone voice a few verses from an ode newly formed in his head . . . one would not shout 'Admirable! Superb! Prodigious!' which had just been used to praise some utter mediocrity. Instead, one would observe a moment of silence and then rise, advance with visible emotion, take the master by the hands, and look heavenward. . . . As the crowd listened with bated breath . . . a single word would be uttered and, to the amazement of those not in the know, echoed and reechoed in every corner of the salon. It was: 'Cathedral!' . . . The speaker then returned to his place, as another entoned: 'Ogive!' A third, after looking about, would hazard: 'Pyramids of Egypt!' Now the assembly applauded, only to fall into a profound contemplation, which was nothing more than preparation for a veritable explosion of voices, all repeating in chorus the sacramental words that had just been pronounced."

Victor Hugo (1802–85)

Still a great cultural force, La Bibliothèque de l'Arsenal possesses an incomparable collection of medieval illuminated manuscripts, saved for the most part from monasteries suppressed during the Revolution, and a unique collection related to the theatre, which includes the archives of Jacques Copeau and Louis Jouvet.

above and opposite: At the Arsenal these rooms are decorated in a Rococo exquisite enough to evoke the name of Germain Boffrand, the style's inventor. But, in all probability, they were created about 1745 by the architect Dauphin for the Duchesse du Maine, whose husband, Louis XIV's natural but legitimatized son, held the position of Grand Master of the Artillery. The Duchess called the room on the opposite page her *salon de musique.* There the beautiful flat-top desk reveals the manner of Boulle; it is surrounded by armchairs made about 1760 for the Marquis de Paulmy, the director of the Arsenal whose passion for books gave the old cannon foundry its first reputation as a library. The delightful *cabinet* above is one of the suite of five rooms occupied by

Dauphin himself during the Maine tenure.   **pages 54–55:** The décor here was created at the Arsenal about 1640, just after the Duc de La Meilleraye, then the Grand Master of the Artillery, had married Marie de Cossé. It consists of surfaces entirely covered with painting: allegorical scenes on the ceiling, and on the walls standing figures of men famous in history. Surrounding the latter are arabesque designs incorporating allegorical figures, sphinxes, birds, beasts, and a whole repertoire of medallions, vases, and musical instruments, all interlinked by garlands of flowers and fruits. In the panels just below are landscapes containing scenes from French history, such as the entry of Henri IV into Paris (1596) and the siege of La Rochelle (1627–28).

Hôtel des Ambassadeurs de Hollande

The Hôtel des Ambassadeurs de Hollande is seriously misnamed, for no amount of research has been able to identify a moment when an envoy from The Netherlands actually resided at this address. Thus it has been called, however, since the 18th century, for in 1752 Blondel, in his *Architecture française,* wrote: "This house has long been inhabited by the ambassador of Holland." It is now thought that the hôtel's name must have arisen from the residence there in the 18th century of a chaplain who, in the service of the Dutch ambassador, provided Protestant services.

The misnomer may also derive from the reluctance of the 17th and 18th centuries to accept the possibility that a bourgeois might have the taste, as well as the money, to commission a house of such splendor. So, rather than call the mansion the Hôtel Amelot, for Denis Amelot de Chaillou, who built it, and Jean-Baptiste Amelot de Bisseuil, who decorated the interior, Parisians of the *ancien régime* possibly preferred to make a connection with a foreign dignitary. The Amelots were in fact of a well-established family belonging to the *noblesse de la robe,* those industrious participants in the French parlements who, dressed in their jurist robes, carried out much of the nation's legal and administrative work.

Socially, therefore, they would have ranked well below the old, land-holding, feudal aristocracy, called the *noblesse de l'épée* for their ancient responsibility to defend the country with arms.

The site of the Hôtel des Ambassadeurs de Hollande is an old one with a history that was rich long before the Amelots arrived. The immediately preceding hôtel dated back to the Hundred Years War (1337–1453), when the householder was the Maréchal de Rieux, a companion in arms of that great hero of the age, Bertrand du Guesclin. Pierre des Rieux, the son of the Marshal, fought alongside Joan of Arc in her campaign to rid France of its English invaders.

Early in the 17th century the old medieval hôtel belonged to François de Hardy, whose wife, Henriette de Coulanges, was the aunt of Madame de Sévigné. It was de Hardy who in 1638 sold the property to

Built about 1650–60 from plans by Pierre Cottard, the Hôtel des Ambassadeurs de Hollande is entered through a majestically Baroque portico surmounted by a round-headed pediment whose tympanum is embellished with sculptural personifications of War and Peace, both carved about 1660 by Thomas Regnaudin.

opposite: At the Hôtel des Ambassadeurs de Hollande the entrance portals bear the richly carved panels of Thomas Regnaudin. They give access to the main courtyard, where the façades are classically sober but embellished by infant terms serving as caryatids for the cornice. The play of light and shadow is further enhanced by the relief in the pilasters flanking the archway, in the robust balustrade above and in the sculptural torches over windows and in the pediment.

below: Between certain of the bays of the upper wall in the main courtyard survive a series of curious old sundials, all designed by Père Truchet, a mathematician and Carmelite friar. At the ground level a vaulted passage leads to an inner courtyard, creating a still more dramatic, and Baroque, contrast of light and dark.

At the Hôtel des Ambassadeurs de Hollande this splendid room *à l'italienne* is a reconstruction recently made from early engravings of Pierre Cottard's original designs (c. 1660). The only 17th-century elements now in the room are the marble fireplace **(below left)** and the illusionistic ceiling painting by Louis de Boullongne: *The Marriage of Hercules and Hebe* **(opposite).** Even the woodwork, with its richly carved garlands, clustered fruits and flowers, monumental atlantes and *putti,* is a modern re-creation. The paintings for the overdoors and the medallions having been lost, they are now replaced with photographic enlargements of drawings by Poussin on the same theme—the story of Hercules—made for the Grande Galerie in the Louvre.

Denis Amelot. The new house that now rose came from plans drawn up by Pierre Cottard. In 1711 the builders' descendants sold the mansion to Claude Miotte, the secretary to Louis XIV at the end of his life. From 1773 to 1788 the Hôtel des Ambassadeurs de Hollande had the great honor to house the dramatist Caron de Beaumarchais, whose *Barber of Seville* (1785) and *Marriage of Figaro* (1784) are among the immortal works of world literature. Although deemed too impertinent toward the aristocracy to be performed on a public stage, the comedies were enjoyed at court, where Marie-Antoinette herself took the role of the deliciously subversive Rosina! Still, the sheer cleverness of Beaumarchais brought him into royal employment as a secret agent, as well as into dealings related to the American Revolution. The playwright now set up in the Hôtel des Ambassadeurs de Hollande the firm of Rodrigue, Horatalès et Cie, which was nothing more than a front financed by France and Spain for the purpose of supplying the American insurgents with arms. But in 1799 the brave and gifted Beaumarchais died impoverished by the failure of the Americans to return payment, as well as by such speculative ventures as a complete edition of the works of Voltaire.

opposite: Thanks to the monumentality of its décor, the gallery in the Hôtel des Ambassadeurs de Hollande appears much larger than its actual, rather modest dimensions: 13 × 39 feet. For the most part the ensemble is a modern reconstruction from engravings contemporary with its creation (c. 1660), but a precious survivor from the 17th century is the painted vault by Michel Corneille. At the center **(left)** he represented "The Apotheosis of Psyche," and at either end "Mercury and Psyche" and "Psyche Carried Off by the Zephyrs." The whole of the ceiling composition required rather extensive restoration and new gilding. Over the fireplace, which is modern work based upon the early engravings, appears *The Toilette of Psyche* by an anonymous 17th-century painter. For the spaces between the windows and doors Corneille painted further scenes representing the adventures of Psyche as told by Apuleius. Now lost, they have been replaced with photographic copies of certain of the *grisaille* figures on the vault.

Within Beaumarchais' own generation another famous author came to the Hôtel des Ambassadeurs de Hollande. Here, in 1766, Germaine, the daughter of the Swiss banker Jacques Necker, was brought to be baptized in the mansion's Protestant chapel. If the financial wizzadry of Necker failed to save the government of Louis XVI, then his daughter, as Madame de Staël, perhaps made up for it in the enrichment her searching, educated, and powerfully critical mind brought to French literature. The nemesis of Napoleon, this brilliant woman wrote most of *De l'allemagne,* that blueprint for the French Romantic movement, not in Paris, which she adored, but in exile at the Château de Chaumont in the Loire Valley.

Dreadfully abused in the 19th century, the Hôtel des Ambassadeurs de Hollande has been under careful restoration for the last twenty-five years. It is now the headquarters of the Paul-Louis Weiller Foundation.

Antonin-Nompar de Caumont, Duc de Lauzun (1633–1723)

Hôtel Lauzun

Of all the famous folk who have lived or been received at the Hôtel Lauzun on the Quai d'Anjou, the one to spend the least time there must surely be Antonin-Nompar de Caumont, Duc de Lauzun, for whom the great mansion has been called since the 19th century. Lauzun did in fact own the house for about three years, from 1682 to 1685, but, as always, he was too peripatetic in his ambition to gain an important army command—an ambition pursued more in the boudoir than on the battlefield—to remain long in a house of his own.

Far more distinguished than Lauzun is the name of the architect to whom the hôtel's plans have always been attributed. Louis Le Vau (1612–20) long ago transcended his role as a major exponent of French Ba-

The façade on the Quai d'Anjou, Île Saint-Louis

he heavily gilded suite of rooms on the main floor

65

roque classicism to enter history as one of the greatest form-givers of all time. And contemporary with the Hôtel Lauzun, Le Vau was also engaged in the designing and building of Vaux-le-Vicomte, often called the finest château in France outside the royal domains. So triumphant was Vaux-le-Vicomte—a complete and totally integrated ensemble of gardens, waterworks, architecture, and sumptuous interior décor—that it seemed fit for no one less than a King. Realizing this, the sponsoring châtelain—the gifted but unwise finance minister Nicolas Fouquet—invited the young Louis XIV to be guest of honor at the château's inauguration in 1661. After touring the gardens and fountains, attending a banquet prepared by the immortal Vatel, enjoying a comedy-ballet specially composed by Moilère and set to the new music of Lully, and after hearing a tribute delivered by the poet La Fontaine and then gasping at fireworks dancing on the "grand canal" and over the château's great dome—after all this the King stormed away from Vaux, outraged that a subject, however highly placed, should dare to outshine the monarch himself. Three weeks later Fouquet was arrested on allegations of embezzlement, and shortly afterwards Le Vau, on royal command, left for Versailles, there to lay out the grand façade fronting upon the immense spread of watered gardens created by Le Nôtre, another and crucial member of Fouquet's creative team at Vaux-le-Vicomte.

Le Vau's patron at the Hôtel Lauzun would have been Charles Gruyn des Bordes, a financier who struck it rich providing hay for the horses of the French army. Gruyn had been a well-known denizen of the Île Saint-Louis and the Île de la Cité, for his father owned La Pomme de Pin ("The Pine Cone"), a cabaret in the Rue de la Juiverie famed for its clientele, which included Rabelais in the 16th century and in the 17th century Molière, Boileau, Racine, and many other of the era's most creative talents. The occasion for the new hôtel commissioned by Gruyn *fils* was his second marriage, to a young widow, Geneviève de Möy, whose cipher can be found repeatedly interlaced with her husband's in the decorations painted on the interior wall paneling. No doubt Gruyn risked being struck down along with Fouquet, to whom he had certain ties, but he survived the difficulties and even regained full grace, for in 1681 the marriage contract of his daughter was signed twice by relations of Colbert, Fouquet's archrival and principal accuser.

After the death of Gruyn, his heirs sold the mansion to Lauzun, who had just returned to Paris from confinement in prison for his attempt to marry La Grande Mademoiselle, a first cousin to Louis XIV. At the court of *le roi soleil* no person of royal blood had any right to a sacramental alliance with a member of the provincial nobility. Not only was Lauzun's brief tenure on the Quai d'Anjou acknowledged mainly in the 19th century, but, in addition, the plaque then placed at the entrance portal mispells the Duke's name as "Lausun" and gives the impossible date of 1657!

In 1685 Lauzun disposed of the house to the Marquis de Richelieu, who three years before had abducted and married Marie-Charlotte de La Meilleraye, daughter of the Duc de La Meilleraye and Hortense Mancini, the niece of Cardinal Mazarin. The Duke, who after the Cardinal's death preferred to be known as the Duc de Mazarin, was a religious bigot with more than one mission, which may account for his daughter's sudden elopement. "On all his estates," says Saint-Simon, "he forbade the women young and old to milk cows, in order to preserve them from all evil thoughts. And because his daughters had nice teeth, he even wanted to have their front ones pulled out for fear they might take pride in them." His wife, who was not altogether happy in his care, led a life of her own. She was most attractive to the son of *le grand* Condé, who spent

The Hôtel Lauzun, built about 1650–58 from plans attributed to the great Louis Le Vau, is marked by an extreme simplicity on its exterior, which makes the rich, gilded interiors seem all the more sumptuous. On the façade overlooking the Quai d'Anjou **(page 65)** only a balcony of superby wrought iron animates the sober composition. The courtyard façades **(opposite)** are even plainer, their elevation consisting of a flattened arcade on the ground level, ordinary rectangular windows just above, a top story of tall windows, which light the reception rooms, and a dormered attic. It was in an apartment on the court—the exact one now unknown—that the poet Charles Baudelaire **(above)** lived for several years after 1842, here beginning *Les Fleurs du mal* and receiving the cream of 19th-century Romantic Paris.

below: The great staircase at the Hôtel Lauzun is a reconstruction brought about in 1935–40. Originally built in the 17th century, the ramps had been destroyed in the early 19th century to make way for a great salon. The painting on the vault—*Truth Revealed by Time*—is attributed to Charles Le Brun, the collaborator of Le Vau and Le Nôtre at Vaux-le-Vicomte and later at Versailles. Over the doors are stucco reliefs of infant groups personifying Music, Poetry, the Sciences, and the Arts. The shell-headed niche on the wall facing the landing contains a statue of Minerva, which corresponds to a niched Apollo on the opposite wall.

opposite: The opulent décor of this room—with its vases, *putti,* and panels filled with flat-pattern, arabesque designs, all on gold grounds occasionally inlaid with blue—reflects the manner current during the early part of Louis XIV's reign. However, modifications made in the early 18th century are the marble mantelpiece and pierglass, which no doubt supplanted decorations comparable to those seen reflected back from the facing wall. The author of the changes is believed to have been the Marquise de Richelieu, whose portrait is enframed high on the wall and whose husband owned the hôtel from 1685 to 1705.

a fortune on her, and another fortune spying on her behavior. Condé, outraged by the favors she granted the Comte de Roucy, was willing to indulge in almost any adventure in order to redeem his honor. Almost but not quite. When his mistress proposed a meeting with Roucy in her own home and added that Condé could easily post his men in hiding and make off with the Count, Condé lost interest. In fact, he told Roucy about the plot and never looked at Madame de Richelieu again. As for the Marquis de Richelieu at the Hôtel Lauzun, "he was an obscure, ruined, and debauched man . . . buried in filth and surrounded by the vilest company, albeit," continued Saint-Simon, "with great spirit."

Still more extravagant things were to happen at the Hôtel Lauzun in the 19th century, but not until a peaceful period had elapsed during which the house was owned, beginning in 1709, by Pierre Ogier, receiver general of the clergy, and then by the Marquis de Pimodan. Finally, the so-called Lauzun mansion entered a phase almost too ripe to describe. In 1842 the person to take possession was the art collector and bibliophile Baron Jérôme Pichon, whose tenant on the ground floor, the now forgotten dandy Roger de Beauvoir, admitted into this Baroque splendor a veritable swarm of Paris' leading Romantics—Delacroix, Musset, Gautier, Dumas *père,* Balzac, and many others. "I have known all the wits of our time," wrote Théophile Gautier, "and I have no hesitation in saying that not one of them was as clever as Roger de Beauvoir. To see him at the dinner table was to see him at his best. Once he had downed two or three glasses of champagne, he was the life of the party." The day Beauvoir moved out, his apartment was taken over by the painter Boissard de Boisdenier, who there founded a club of hashish smokers. Gautier, himself an enthralled addict and a tenant of the Hôtel Lauzun for a while, noted the club members' "bright eyes and the flushed cheeks beneath the swollen veins of their temples."

Gautier also tells about the most illustrious of all the hôtel's occupants—the *poète maudit* Charles Baudelaire. "The first time I met Baudelaire was about the middle of 1845, when I had a fancy apartment communicating with his by a hidden staircase in the wall, and doubtless haunted by the ghost of the fair ladies the Duc de Lauzun made love to in the old days." Little more is known about the suite occupied by Baudelaire. One of the few descriptions of it we owe to Théodore de Banville, who admired "the atmosphere of voluptuous and aggressive elegance" and noticed that it contained "no study nor writing table, no sideboard and no dining room, in fact nothing to recall the well-defined divisions of a middle-class apartment. . . . He invited me to have lunch with him, and at once, as if by magic, the table was laid and succulent dishes served by a silent manservant." Baudelaire's biographer Charles Asselineau records that on the wall there was a small version of Delacroix's *Women of Algiers,* a present from the artist, and also a portrait of Baudelaire by Émile Deroy, who made it, according to the artist, "in three or four evenings, by the light of a smoky lamp, in 1843." This means that the picture was painted on the Quai d'Anjou, for the poet had moved there in 1842. And no doubt it was here that he composed the first pieces for *Les Fleurs du mal.*

On the death of Baron Pichon in 1899 the city of Paris acquired the Hôtel Lauzun, then retroceded it to his grandson, Baron Louis Pichon, who rebuilt the staircase demolished in the 19th century, then went on to make certain unwarranted additions of his own. When he died in 1928, the city of Paris took command of the property once again. Now the French government uses the house as a residence for distinguished guests from abroad.

left above and below: Reigning over the Hôtel Lauzun's former *chambre de parade* (a kind of state bedroom) is a painted ceiling of incredible decorative wealth. At the center is an airy, oval composition entitled *The Triumph of Venus,* enframed by figures, full-color scenes, and *grisaille* medallions, all represented in *trompe l'oeil* on the coved surface of the vault. Thematically, everything on the perifery extends and explains the event seen at the center. Eighteenth-century additions to the room are the fireplace and the mirrors. The gallery reflected in the mirror, a fanciful creation of the early 20th century, replaced what originally was an alcove. **opposite:** Here is the original 17th-century decoration of the wall facing that reproduced on page 69.

pages 72–73: The Hôtel Lauzun's 17th-century boudoir is positively encrusted with richly carved and gilded moldings enframing painted decorative panels, all crowned by a veritable explosion of arabesque garlands intertwined with voluptuous nudes and converging upon the central illusionistic composition: *Zephyr and Flora.* The mirrors, which date from the 18th century when such things were extremely costly, follow the fashion that culminated in the great Hall of Mirrors at Versailles.

Hôtel Lambert

"There is every likelihood that on our return from the Low Countries we shall settle in Paris," wrote Voltaire to the future Frederick the Great in the spring of 1739. "Madame du Châtelet has just purchased a house built by one of the greatest architects in France [Le Vau] and decorated by Le Brun and Le Sueur. It is the very house for a sovereign who would also be a philosopher. Fortunately it is in a neighborhood far removed from everything. For this reason two million francs could purchase a house that cost two million just to build and decorate. I look upon it as a second retreat, a second Cirey." But despite this expression of enthusiasm for the Hôtel Lambert, Voltaire was not one to demand a superb setting. He worshiped luxury but only in a platonic manner, as anyone can tell who has visited either Les Délices, his town house in Geneva, or Ferney, his nearby villa just beyond the Swiss frontier in France. The Château de Cirey, the estate in Champagne of his mistress, Madame du Châtelet, where he lived on an off for sixteen years, was comfortable and aristocratic but far from splendid.

The retreat offered by the Hôtel Lambert was one that Voltaire would have scant opportunity to explore. The great writer was just entering one of the more agitated periods in his life. Soon he would accompany Madame du Châtelet to Brussels, where she was contesting a law-

above: Access to Le Vau's Hôtel Lambert (1640–44), at the bottom of the courtyard, is made unusually graceful by the concave transition leading to the entrance pavilion, where the open double-stair vestibule is recessed behind a Doric colonnade. All is plain, sober, and classical, but lightened by the windows, which are exceptionally large for a 17th-century structure. The ground-floor windows on the right of the courtyard illuminate the grand salon **(opposite)**. On this interior the beautiful *boiseries* were installed in the 18th century. They now provide an elegant setting for a stunning collection of art works and objects. Of particular note are the paintings by Dutch masters on either side of the fireplace, the gilded bronze pieces, and rare small cupboards designed by Carlin. The medal cabinet in the foreground came from the atelier of Roetgen.

suit. For three years now he had been in correspondence with Crown Prince Frederick of Prussia, and in 1740 he would go to Berlin, leaving behind his mistress, annoyed and jealous. Furthermore, Voltaire was campaigning for a seat at the Academy, which he failed to obtain, but a different kind of success came with *Mérope,* performed in 1743. Altogether, Voltaire was to spend only five weeks at the Hôtel Lambert and had to wait until 1742 for the privilege. Thus, he commented: "While the town house of the Marquise du Châtelet is unquestionably one of the finest in Paris, it has always had for me the charm of a castle in Spain, because I have only lived in it from a distance."

The Hôtel Lambert was undertaken in 1640 by Louis Le Vau for Jean-Baptiste Lambert de Thorigny, the most successful son of a successful financier. On Lambert's death in 1644, at age thirty-three, the foundations had been laid and the walls put in place, which left the job of completing and decorating the building to Lambert's younger

above: For the Hôtel Lambert, Le Vau very skillfully made the most of the site, the tip end of the Île Saint-Louis. The wing on the right projects from the main mass of the building to give access from the grand salon to the gardens on one side **(above)** and to the courtyard on the other (page 75). The garden forms a terrace leading to the Seine embankment. Behind the façade on the right is found the celebrated Galerie d'Hercule **(opposite and page 78).** There the ceiling decoration—an illusionistic painting of the Apotheosis of Hercules—was the first major commission undertaken by Le Brun, who went on to become the chief decorator of Louis XIV's Versailles. Jacques Rousseau did the arcadian landscapes in the bays opposite the windows, while on the intervening wall sections van Obstal executed the stucco atlantes and sphinxes sustaining the alternately oval and octagonal medallions representing the Feats of Hercules.

below: Revised on several occasions, the décor of the library in the Hôtel Lambert retains some 17th-century elements in the panels framing the shelves. The mantelpiece and its pierglass date from the 18th century. Also to this period belong the candelabra and the remarkable clock with its sculptural representation of the Rape of Europa. The painting is the great portrait of Baroness Betty de Rothschild by Ingres.

pages 80–81: The Salon des Cuirs, or "Leather Drawing Room," is hung with a series of paintings on Cordovan leather that date from c. 1660 and have been attributed to Rembrandt. The scenes represent "The Triumphal Entry of David into Jerusalem after the Victory over Goliath." On the table is a collection of nautilus shells mounted in Augsburg at the beginning of the 17th century. The tankard in the foreground is made of ivory and silver molded in relief to depict *putti*, shells, and dolphins. The two small salons seen on page 81 have recently been fitted out in the manner of the *cabinets de curiosités* so dear to the collectors of the Renaissance. The rooms now contain a magnificent series of Limousin painted enamels and objects in Italian majolica, most of which are from the 16th century.

brother, Nicolas, who called on Charles Le Brun, later famous for his monumental achievements at Versailles, to paint the ceiling depicting the labors of Hercules. This work, according to the English scholar Anthony Blunt, became the most ambitious piece of Baroque illusionism so far realized in France. When it came to the Cabinet des Muses and the Cabinet de l'Amour, Lambert counted on Eustache Le Sueur, himself a major artist of the French Early Baroque. The Cabinet des Muses was to be altered in the 18th century and some of its paintings removed. These are now in the Louvre. As for the Cabinet de l'Amour, it has been stripped of its paneling, as well as of its original paintings.

In 1682 Nicolas Lambert married his son to the daughter of Bontemps, the chief *valet de chambre* to Louis XIV and the confidant of the King's amours. The Lambert heirs retained the hôtel until 1732, when it passed to the rich tax collector Claude Dupin, who also owned the great Château de Chenonceaux in the Loire Valley. The beautiful Madame Dupin is well known to posterity from the frequent references made to her by Jean-Jacques Rousseau in his *Confessions.* In 1746, several years after the Dupins had given up the Hôtel Lambert, Jean-Jacques entered the Dupin household as a kind of secretary to Madame and as a tutor to her children. This was four years before the Academy of Dijon awarded him first prize for his essay proving that the cultivation of science and the arts inevitably provoked a decline in morals. The essay was a sensation, prompting a friend to argue that the author had been wasting his time with Madame Dupin. Rousseau did not share the opinion. Indeed he adored Madame Dupin, and greatly appreciated the opportunity she provided to speak about his children by his mistress, Thérèse Levasseur, all of whom had been dispatched to a foundling home. "When I saw [Madame Dupin] for the first time," wrote Jean-Jacques, "she was still one of the most beautiful women in Paris. She received me while getting dressed. She had nothing over her arms; her hair was disheveled, and her dressing gown in disarray. This came as something new to me. I was confused. I was bewildered. In short, there I was in love with her."

Madame du Châtelet acquired the Hôtel Lambert from the Dupins in 1739, let it out to the Portuguese ambassador in 1744, and the next year sold the mansion to the tax collector Martin de La Haye. At this owner's death in 1776, the Comte d'Angivilliers was able to acquire some of the paintings by Le Sueur. In 1781 the hôtel passed to Barthélemy Davenne-Desfontaine, who in 1813 sold it to Comte de Montalivet, minister of the interior under the Empire. This proprietor, after transferring what remained of the Cabinet de l'Amour decorations to his château, divested himself of the house in 1816. Finally, in 1843, the mansion went to an owner capable of appreciating Le Vau's superb architecture. This was the Polish Prince Adam Czartorisky, exiled from his native land for having pleaded with Czar Alexander I to restore the Kingdom of Poland. The Czartoriskys led a charmed life at the Hôtel Lambert, often giving splendid *fêtes.* Ladislas, Prince Adam's eldest son, married Princess Amparo, born of the morganatic marriage of Maria Christina, Queen of Spain, with the Duke of Rianzanares. The new Princess Czartoriska was an intimate of the Empress Eugénie, herself a Spanish Princess, who called at the Hôtel Lambert to pray over her friend when she lay dying. In his second marriage Prince Ladislas took as his wife the Princess Marguerite-Adélaïde d'Orléans, daughter of the Duc de Nemours and the granddaughter of King Louis-Philippe.

Recently sold by the Czartoryskis, the Hôtel Lambert has now been restored by the present owner, Baron Guy de Rothschild, who has filled Le Vau's great rooms with a truly fabulous collection of paintings, furniture, enamel, faience, Renaissance jewelry, and other antiquities.

above and opposite: At the Hôtel Lambert the décor of the Cabinet des Muses was originally executed by Le Sueur. This master's ceiling composition—*Phaeton Asking Apollo to Lend Him His Chariot*—remains in place, but the large paintings for the walls—devoted to the Muses—were removed in 1776 and, after entering the royal collections, are now in the Louvre. Replacing them are 17th-century still life and flower paintings. The cartouche decorations, although attributed to Le Sueur, seem to have been radically modified about 1700 in the manner of Berain and Audran.

The Faubourg Saint-Germain

Hôtel de Luzy

Hôtel Gouffier de Thoix

Hôtel de Brienne

Hôtel de Galliffet

Hôtel Matignon

Hôtel du Châtelet

Hôtel de Boisgelin

Hôtel de Beauharnais

Hôtel de Roquelaure

Hôtel de Saint-Simon

Hôtel de Salm-Dyck

Hôtel Séguier

Hôtel de Salm

Hôtel d'Avaray

At the Hôtel de Roquelaure, a detail of
the Rococo interior décor

Hôtel de Luzy

The presence of a Picasso, not to mention the silk screens of Andy Warhol, may seem an impertinence in the Hôtel de Luzy, but an impertinence that is quickly subdued by the cool elegance of the interiors, which cannot but evoke the Louis XVI style in that moment of equilibrium when Christoph Willibald von Gluck, the serene classicist and Marie-Antoinette's favorite composer, was conquering Paris with his first opera in French: *Iphigénie en Tauride* (1779). Structually, however, the great house now called the Hôtel de Luzy dates back to the late 17th century; thus, it was the drastic remodeling of 1770 that gave the building its calm elegance. Historically, the hôtel became notable only in 1772, when Charles-Maurice de Talleyrand-Périgord, then an eighteen-year-old seminarian, developed an interest in Dorothée Dorinville, a comely actress of twenty-five currently engaged at the Comédie-Française. Without mentioning her name, which professionally was Mademoiselle de Luzy, the old and celebrated Duc de Talleyrand wrote in his *Mémoires:* "I had reached the age when the passions as well as the mysteries of the spirit begin to reveal themselves, at the moment in life when every faculty is alert and active. Now, on several occasions, I had noticed in a chapel at Saint-Sulpice a lovely young person whose simple and modest air pleased me very much. At eighteen, if one is not depraved, it is those qualities that attract. I began to attend services more regularly. One day as she was leaving, a

above: Here, in another view of the Hôtel de Luzy's ground-floor salon, this spacious room is seen to be illuminated by four tall windows opening to the garden on one side and to the courtyard on the other. The small adjacent sitting room **(opposite),** having lost the whole of its 18th-century décor, is now hung with green velvet, which serves as a dramatic foil to a painting by Picasso and to a quadruple portrait of the house's mistress by Andy Warhol. The bronzes and other objects on the tables date from the 16th and 17th centuries.

heavy shower gave me the courage to see her home, provided she did not live too far away. She accepted to share my umbrella, and I accompanied her to the Rue Férou, where she lived. She then allowed me to come in, and, with all the guilelessness of the pure in heart, she urged me to come again. At first I called every three or four days, then more often. Against the young lady's own wishes, her parents had made her study acting. And I, against my own nature, found myself in the seminary. Our respective dilemmas provided a bond and allowed us to confide in one another without reserve. Her troubles and mine filled our conversations. I have been told since that she lacked cleverness, but I was never aware of this defect, even after two years of seeing her daily."

Sixteen years later Talleyrand would be consecrated Bishop of Autun, but religion was never an obsession with him. "One simply has to be rich," he was fond of saying. Naturally, he would withdraw from the Church in 1791, for Talleyrand was destined to become the diplomatic master of Europe. As for the first love Talleyrand could not forget—the

below: At the Hôtel de Luzy the hall leading to the library has been arranged as an imitation garden pavilion built of trellises, with mirrors used to reflect the actual garden outside. Set up over a niched basin is a late 18th-century fountain figure made of terracotta. In the library itself **(opposite)** the bookcases are veneered in tortoiseshell and trimmed with stainless-steel moldings. The floor too is steel-plated, and in part covered by a rug whose "marbled" pattern echoes the mottled coloration of the tortoiseshell. Except for two small tables in marquetry by André-Charles Boulle (1642–1732), the furniture is almost all of the Louis XVI period. Over the fireplace hangs a portrait of the house's master by the English painter Graham Sutherland.

sweet tenant of the Hôtel de Luzy—she was also remembered by the tragedienne Mademoiselle Clairon: "Her figure was elegant and so were her features . . . her bearing noble, her gestures quite tolerable, her pronunciation excellent." At the Comédie-Française she made her debut in 1763 as Dorine in Molière's *Tartuffe*. A Jewess, she converted to Catholicism, which, along with her indifference to moral strictness, prompted another actress, Sophie Arnould, to declare: "She made herself a Christian when she found that God had made himself a man."

During the 19th century the Hôtel de Luzy passed from one owner to another. By the end of World War II it was in a state of dilapidation, but now has been beautifully restored by its present owner.

opposite: The boudoir on the second level at the Hôtel de Luzy is saved from its actual corridorlike narrowness by two large windows, one giving onto the courtyard and the other onto the garden, and by a pair of wall mirrors, which, by facing one another, have the effect of multiplying the space into infinity. Mirrors also line the niches, while the décor is otherwise completed by blue and white Chinese porcelains and by Louis XVI armchairs whose soft-blue upholstery matches the color of the draperies.   **left:** The cloakroom is of an extremely fine décor, consisting of stucco reliefs of vases and flowers rendered in an Oriental style and set against a ground of lapis blue framed by imitation green malachite. Here again, mirrors give the illusion of compounded space and create a powerful sense of fantasy.

opposite: The former reception room of Mademoiselle de Luzy has now become a dining room. Still intact is the 18th-century white and gold paneling carved with flower garlands and, over each door, a pair of cupids holding an antique incense burner. Similar incense burners have been found and placed on plinths between the windows. The Louis XVI furniture includes two ebony-veneered console tables in designs that originated in the 17th century. Through a door **(above)** can be seen one of the niches in the boudoir illustrated on the preceding page. It contains a collection of fine Chinese porcelain.

Hôtel Gouffier de Thoix

The entrance portal on the street is the finest part of the architecture for the Hôtel Gouffier de Thoix. A sculptural glory, the tympanum has been carved with a profusion of scallops, conches, and other varieties of shell, all treated with an astonishing realism. Also carved and beautifully executed are the door panels, which bear a relief composition of medallions containing figures of Mars and Minerva and surrounded by antique trophies and helmets.

No architect's name has been attached to the Hôtel Gouffier de Thoix, but the luxurious charm of its doorway opens into a good example of the quiet elegance that obtained on this street throughout the 18th century. And the neighborhood lost none of its appeal for at least two distinguished authors of our time. Edith Wharton maintained an apartment at 53 bis, Rue de Varenne, while André Gide had his flat around the corner at 1 bis, Rue Vaneau.

The mansion was built by Henriette Penancoët de Kéroualle, wife of Thimoléon Gouffier, Marquis de Thoix, on land she acquired in 1719. The wealth of Madame de Thoix had its origin in her fortuitous position as sister of Louise de Kéroualle, who with the encouragement and gratitude of Louis XIV became Duchess of Portsmouth and the mistress of Charles II, thus an agent for France in England at the most intimate level. And Henriette herself knew something of the land north of the Channel, for in her first marriage she had been Countess of Pembroke.

In 1768 Henriette's grandson sold the town house to Antoine-Martin Chaumont de La Galaizière, whose father, a grain merchant, had got splendidly rich in the days of the Regency (1715–23), when the Scottish speculator John Law founded the Compagnie des Indes so as to capitalize on the attractions of Louisiana. Through "Law's system" sudden fortunes could be made and lost, and in the process a cook might turn up at the opera in a seat next to his master. Such was the fortune gained by La Galaizière that it seemed hardly touched even after a court judgment required him to restore some eight million francs to the government in 1722. As for young Antoine-Martin, the owner of the Hôtel Gouffier de Thoix, he had the wit to marry the daughter of Jean Orry, who had made a fortune of his own reforming the administration of Philip V of Spain. But money seemed to be the family's stock in trade, for Philibert Orry, Antoine-Martin's brother-in-law, was for fifteen years France's controller of finances under Louis XV.

These powerful relations explain how, in 1738, Antoine-Martin de La Galaizière was appointed chancellor of the Lorraine under Stanislas Leczinski, the dethroned King of Poland. His true employer, of course, was Stanislas' son-in-law, Louis XV, but as an administrator he appears to have been able and appreciated, relieving the reigning Duc de Lorraine of all governmental duties. He also relieved the old monarch of his young and charming mistress, the Marquise de Boufflers. Jean Orieux,

in his *Voltaire*, reports that the affair of the mistress shared by two lovers was well regulated in the civilized manner of the 18th century. One evening, for instance, the Marquise, somewhat sated with endearments from the elderly Stanislas, responded at last by saying: "Is that all?" To which the King replied: "No, Madame, it is not all, by my Chancellor will tell you the rest!"

After Madame de La Galaizière died, the Chancellor returned to Paris from the Lorraine, and it was then, in 1761, that he acquired the Hôtel Gouffier de Thoix. In 1782 the house went to his son, who emigrated during the Revolution, causing the property to be seized. After passing through a variety of hands in the 19th century, the mansion remains a private residence.

left: One of the salons in the Hôtel Gouffier de Thoix retains its late 18th-century paneling painted a sober white and gilded in the restricted areas of the mirror frames and the crowning laurel-leaf friezes. Of all the furniture collected here, especially fine are the roll-top desk in the style of Oeben and the *voyeuse* or "observation chair." Often confused with the *prie-Dieu,* this curious piece of furniture was made for ladies wanting to kneel while watching a game of cards. The kneeler could lean forward on the upholstered upper ledge of the chair's back. **opposite:** In the dining room a monumental niche is crowned with a laurel wreath and a pair of cornucopias spilling out fruits and flowers. Like the carving at the entrance portal, these forms have been executed with a marked degree of naturalism. The richly sculptural terracotta stove that fills the niche is in the finest Rococo style. A modification made during the Empire (1804–14) affected only the base. Porcelains and the gilded clock brighten a perfect 18th-century ensemble, which is completed by the leather-upholstered Louis XV chairs.

opposite: The *boiseries* in the Hôtel Gouffier de Thoix, while regrettably scraped down, reflect the Régence style at its best, especially in the "mosaicized" panels and in the relief compositions of trophies and musical instruments. Furniture and objets d'art dating mostly from the 17th and 18th centuries are admirably integrated into a setting of great elegance. The small brackets on the panels flanking the fireplace mirror are unusual pieces made of Cantonese enamel and mounted in bronze at the beginning of the 18th century.

above: In the boudoir the bed, as always in the old houses, occupies the place of honor. Here the bed has been crowned *à la polonaise*— that is, with an imperial dome sustained by wrought-iron mounts, which are concealed by the draperies.

Hôtel de Brienne

François Debias-Aubry has never been a name to conjure with, even though its bearer had considerable success in his own time—the first half of the 18th century. Critics have often noted that he was not an unworthy student of the art of Jules Hardouin-Mansart, Louis XIV's favorite architect, and the elegant Hôtel de Brienne stands in witness to this judgment. Still, Debias-Aubry failed when he tried to gain admission to the prestigious French Academy in 1737. And as for the Hôtel de Brienne, much of its splendor came with later revisions, which made the present large mansion from what originally were two adjacent but independent houses, both designed by Debias-Aubry, and which transformed many of the Rococo interiors into a Napoleonic conception of Roman imperial grandeur. The name by which we know the hôtel is also the product of a later age, that of the years leading to the French Revolution, when the Comte de Brienne lived at 14–16 Rue Saint-Dominique.

The Comte de Clermont had the initial structure built in 1724, only to sell it the following year to Françoise de Mailly, the widow of Louis de Phélypeaux, Marquis de La Vrillière, who was to marry the Duc de Mazarin in 1731. But if this lady has a place in history, it is thanks to the tragicomic character of her first marriage, the details of which were recorded, with his usual acerbic relish, by the Duc de Saint-Simon: "Only twelve years old, she began to weep and proclaim her unhappiness, most of all to beg them to give her a poor man if necessary, provided only that he be a gentleman, and a not a *petit bourgeois* forced upon her for the sake of his fortune. She was furious with her mother and with Madame de Maintenon [the morganatic and puritanical wife of Louis XIV in his old age] for having arranged the alliance. It was impossible either to appease or quieten her, or to prevent her scowling at La Vrillière and his family, all of whom flocked to inspect the bride-to-be and her mother. . . . But the bargain had been made, too good a bargain to be broken. . . . Everyone hoped that the problem would clear up in time . . . but in fact the young woman never did adjust to being Madame de La Vrillière, and often she let this be known."

After surviving her second husband, the Duchesse de Mazarin sold the house in 1733 to Louise-Élisabeth de Bourbon-Condé, the dowager Princesse de Conti, whose husband's ancestry could be traced back to the brother of Louis XIV's great general, *le grand* Condé. Following the example of her mother—the Duchesse de Bourbon, the legitimatized daughter of Louis XIV and Madame de Montespan, who cultivated an idyllic love, in the nearby Palais Bourbon, with Monsieur de Lassay—the Princesse de Conti maintained a long liaison with the Comte d'Agenais, the son of the Marquise de Richelieu. It was this lady who had been the mistress of the Hôtel Lauzun as well as of the Princesse de Conti's own grandfather, the Prince de Condé!

The subject of the Princesse de Conti's amours is inexhaustible, but more interesting for our purposes is the fact that it was this occupant of

the Hôtel de Brienne who increased the size of the house by adding to it the property next door held by the Abbé de Broglie. The Princess also endowed the interiors with much sumptuous decoration.

At the death of the Princesse de Conti in 1775 the hôtel passed to her great-nephew, the Comte de La Marche, who a year later sold it to Louis-Athanase de Loménie, Comte de Brienne. In 1787–88, the very eve of the fall of the Bastille (1789), this owner became minister of war under Louix XVI, an appointment that took him to the scaffold in 1794. Confiscated and sold, the Hôtel de Brienne was first let to and then acquired by Napoleon's brother, Lucien Bonaparte, in 1802. Lucien, a widower, lived there with his children and his sister Elisa. He also maintained a mistress, Madame Jouberthon, whom he lodged in a house on the neighboring Place du Palais Bourbon. An underground passage connecting the family mansion to the love nest soon became known as the "conjugal subway." The couple's marriage in 1803 infuriated Napoleon, by then First Consul, which caused Lucien and his wife to flee to Italy.

Promptly, the Hôtel de Brienne was claimed and occupied by the estranged brothers' mother—the famous Madame Mère. "She is like a woman of ancient Rome," declared Napoleon, "always above any revolution." After having borne many trials and tribulations with exemplary courage, she had become the mother of an Emperor. Given the title of Imperial Highness by her son, she had an income of a million francs a month. In addition to the Hôtel de Brienne, Madame Mère was the mistress of the Grand Trianon at Versailles. Her household consisted of a head chaplain (the Bishop of Vercelli) and two assistant chaplains, a lady-in-waiting and four lady's companions (including the Duchesse d'Abrantès), two chamberlains, two equerries, and a private secretary (the future Duc Decazes). For her exalted station, Madame Mère was appointed "Patroness General of the Benevolence and Charity Funds of the Empire." But did the old lady enjoy all these titles and splendors? Hardly, for in fact she lived in daily fear of fresh upheavals. "If only the game will last," she used to say again and again, marking every word with the strong Corsican accent that she never lost, and never wished to lose. Frugal from former necessity, she now became miserly for fear of the future. To the Emperor she would say: "If ever I have you on my hands again, you will be grateful for the savings I now contrive to make."

At the Hôtel de Brienne Madame Mère led a quiet, retiring life, in the company of her brother, Cardinal Fresch, and a few priests. They spent their evenings playing a card game called *reversis,* the "eternal reversis" that so annoyed Napoleon. Usually the small company gathered in some gloomy drawing room with the meagerest fire in the grate. But "one evening," writes the historian Lacour-Gayet, "a strange gentleman entered the drawing room of the Hôtel de Brienne. He was wearing evening dress embroidered with silver. It was the Prefect of Paris dressed to go out. He paid no attention to two ladies sitting in a dark corner, talking in low voices. With the utmost composure he warmed his back at the fireplace. Surprised by his unceremonious behavior, one of the ladies finally got up. It was the Baronne de Fleurieu, a lady-in-waiting. 'Do you know, sir, where you are?' she asked. 'Isn't this the house of the Archchancellor?' 'No, it's the home of Madame.' 'Madame who?' 'The home of Madame Mère!' 'But whose mother do you mean?' 'You are in the home of Her Imperial Highness, Madame Mère, the mother of His Majesty the Emperor.' " The Prefect could not have been too intelligent, for he was surrounded by a magnificent décor in the highest Empire style.

Following Napoleon's abdication in 1814, the Hôtel de Brienne became the official residence of France's minister of war, which it remains.

Madame Mère (1750–1836)

Lucien Bonaparte (1770–1840)

opposite: At the Hôtel de Brienne the vestibule and the grand staircase occupy the whole of the central bay and the left portion of the main pavilion facing the court. Particularly noteworthy is the magnificent 18th-century wrought-iron handrail. Both the portrait of Cardinal Richelieu, by Philippe de Champaigne, and that of Napoleon crossing the Alps, by Jacques-Louis David, are early replicas of the original canvases, both of which are in the Louvre.

below: The so-called "Blue Salon" is the only room in the Hôtel de Brienne that retains the superb Rococo paneling installed in the house after 1732 for the Princesse de Conti. Against a pale cream ground a pattern of straight line moldings and curvilinear embellishments has been carved in relief and then brightened with gilt to make an elegant, decorative articulation of wall and door panels, overdoor courtouches, and coved transitions from wall to ceiling. Shell and floral motifs permit discreet flourishes of abstract arabesque design, which makes a particularly subtle contrast to the pure white tonality and naturalism of the overdoor stucco reliefs representing children at play. Frolicking among the sinuous tendrils of the frieze are birds and fanciful animals.   opposite: Like most of the house, the dining room was completely redone during the First Empire (1804–14) for Letizia Bonaparte, the mother of Napoleon who by protocol was known as Madame Mère. Originally, however, the tapestry was one depicting "The Procession of a Triumphant Warrior," but the hanging that has now replaced it represents "The Capture of Dole by Louis XIV." Otherwise, the décor has all the severe, Roman, "imperial" grandeur cultivated in the days of Napoleon's domination of Europe. Typically "Empire," the tapestry-covered chairs belonged to Count Walewski (1810–68), the natural son of the Emperor and his great Polish love, the Countess Maria Walewska. On the consoles as well as on the central table rests a portion of a set of gilt-bronze ware, consisting altogether of thirty-four pieces, made by the goldsmith Pierre-Philippe Thomire (1751–1843).

above: Installed within the Hôtel de Brienne is a particularly fine collection of Empire furniture and objets d'art, much of which belonged to Madame Mère. On the console table seen here stand two gilt and patinated bronze candelabra held aloft by statuettes representing an ephebe and a nymph. They flank a blue porcelain Sèvres vase mounted in gilt bronze.   **opposite:** The focal point of this drawing room is a chimney piece made of polychrome marble. It supports an elaborate clock and houses a rare set of period andirons formed liked antique incense burners. Decorated with rams' heads, the harp is an unusually fine example of an instrument much favored in the Neoclassical era, with its romantic attachment to all things suggestive of Greco-Roman antiquity.

Hôtel de Galliffet

above: The Hôtel de Galliffet was built in 1784–90 from plans by Legrand, who inevitably reflected the growing taste for a Neoclassicism of the most rigorous, even severe, purity. On the garden side illustrated here, short side wings flank a main façade whose principal adornment is a colossal, engaged Ionic colonnade supporting the plainest of entablatures. Above the cornice rises a low attic, while on the ground floor of the wings columns again structure the elevation, as Doric galleries, open on the right side and closed on the left.   **opposite:** A lighter, gayer mood prevails on the interior, especially in the former *chambre de parade* ("state bedroom"), where monumental engaged columns and a heavily carved cornice enframe walls beautifully stuccoed with decorative themes derived from Pompeii, the discovery of which did much to fuel the whole Neoclassical movement. So successful was this décor that Legrand repeated it in the Hôtel de Jarnac.

The sincere if ponderous façade of the Hôtel de Galliffet, which dates from 1784–90, derived from designs by Jacques-Guillaume Legrand, who made his reputation in 1781 with the wooden dome he and his partner, Jacques Molinos, placed atop the Halle au Blé ("Grain Market"). The structure constituted one of the engineering marvels of the age, and it impressed no one more than Thomas Jefferson. The commission for the hôtel—truly a palace—originated with Simon-Alexandre, Marquis de Galliffet, president of the parlement of Provence at the end of the *ancien régime*. Hardly had the house been built when it was confiscated in 1792 as the property of an émigré. The Revolutionary government then made it the headquarters of the Ministry of Foreign Affairs. In the beginning a council of four citizens directed the ministry, but with the fall of Robespierre on 9 Thermidor (July 27, 1794), a single appointee—Charles Delacroix—took charge. Soon, however, Delacroix would be replaced by one of the period's most ubiquitous and enduring personalities—Charles-Maurice, Duc de Talleyrand-Périgord, who, it seems, supplanted Delacroix not only at the Foreign Ministry but also in the good graces of Madame Delacroix. Consequently, it has always been assumed that, while legally the heir of the Revolutionary politician whose name he bore, the great painter Eugène Delacroix, born in 1798, was in fact the son of Talleyrand. Even so, the artist's genius may have come from his mother, whose father, after all, had been J.F. Oeben, one of the foremost *ébénistes* of the Louis XV era.

As for his mother, Talleyrand claimed she "never said a clever thing in all her life." But if there was a lesson in this, Talleyrand learned it early and was rarely less than absolutely certain of his wit as well as his footing—even though, like Byron, he was clubfooted from infancy. "I have found out," he observed, "that certain people think there is something wrong about accepting positions in times of crisis and revolution, when the absolute good is impossible of achievement. It has always seemed to me that there was something superficial in that way of looking at things. In the affairs of the world, the present moment is not the only one to be considered. *What is* really doesn't amount to much, if one doesn't stop to think that *what is* produces *what will be,* and, to tell the truth, if you want to get anywhere, you have to keep moving."

Keep moving Talleyrand did. Thinking more of his physical disability than of his natural proclivities, his family had forced him into a seminary, which in 1789, the year the Bastille fell, led to his being appointed Bishop of Autun by Louis XVI. "It will improve him," commented the misguided monarch. Even Talleyrand's mother had difficulty visualizing a mitre upon her son's head. Whatever the personal improvement, it seems to have taken effect more at the gaming table, for twice Talleyrand broke the bank, both times just after celebrating Mass! In 1791, as the Revolution gathered, he left the Church. Then, to survive the Terror, he fled to England and finally to the United States, where his only consolation seems to have been the friendship of Alexander Hamilton. But he could also write to an alter ego, Madame de Staël: "Another year over here, and I shall be a dead man." A life-long friend, Madame de Staël saw to it that Talleyrand's name was removed from the list of the banished. "You've done absolutely everything I asked for," he wrote her from America. "I love you with all my heart."

Once Talleyrand was back in Paris in the summer of 1797, Madame de Staël next took on the struggle to have her friend appointed to the Foreign Ministry. First, she introduced him to Paul, Vicomte de Barras, a leading power in the Directory. Her argument was that Talleyrand had all the vices of the *ancien régime* and of the *nouveau régime* as well, which would give him entree to every political party. "For that reason," she stated, "you can't possibly find a more useful agent. Besides, since he'll be completely dependent upon your favor, he'll have to take his orders from you." But despite her powers of persuasion, Madame de Staël failed to gain anything for her protégé until she had made a sixth desperate visit to Barras in the Palais du Luxembourg, with Talleyrand waiting outside in a coach. "Entering," wrote Barras, "she flung herself into a chair, dragged me to her—indeed almost upon her—and, all out of breath, she clutched my hands violently: 'Barras . . . Barras . . . How could you let him jump into the Seine for the want of an opportunity to serve his country! No, you will not do this! You must have grit and reveal some character. You must make Talleyrand Foreign Minister; otherwise, I myself shall die of despair, for I am at the end of my rope!' She truly was having convulsions, like someone on the verge of an epileptic seizure, with mouth all afoam." Such were the burlesque beginnings of one of the period's most spectacular careers, which kept Talleyrand at the head of France's Foreign Ministry from 1797 until 1807, except for a short interruption in 1799. His own genius, however, made him the dominant presence at the Congress of Vienna (1814–15), despite the allied defeat of Napoleonic France, and then returned him to favor under both the Bourbons and the Orleanist Louis-Philippe.

Seeing straws in the wind, Talleyrand on January 3, 1798, offered a sumptuous reception at the Hôtel de Galliffet in honor of "Madame Bonaparte," whose young husband had just covered himself with glory in

Charles-Maurice, Duc de Talleyrand-Périgord
(1754–1838)

the Italian campaigns. Both the *diable boiteux* and the military hero seemed to sense from the start that they were two of a kind. "At my first sight of him," wrote Talleyrand in his *Mémoires,* "he struck me as a charming figure. Victory in twenty battles goes so well with youth. Then there were his fine eyes, his pale brow, and a vague sense of having gone to physical excess. The first conversation was, on his part, one of unreserved trust. He said to me: "You are the nephew of the Archbishop of Reims, who in [in exile] with Louis XVIII.' And he added: 'I too have a clergyman uncle, an Archdeacon in Corsica. It was he who brought me up. In Corsica an archdeacon is rather like a Bishop in France.' " Thereupon the two men went into the salons at the Hôtel de Galliffet, where Talleyrand had gathered a choice company.

Toward Madame de Staël, who of course was there, Napoleon displayed conspicuous disregard. This simply intensified the determination of that brilliant and passionate woman to have her own experience of the Romantic age's most romantic figure. In his *Mémoires* the dramatist Arnaud describes another occasion when Madame de Staël attempted to engage Napoleon's attention: "One can't get near the General. Thus, you must present me." But Arnaud hesitated, "fearful of her domineering personality." This very factor, however, forced him to give way and approach Napoleon with Madame de Staël in tow: "The circle tightened around us, with everyone curious to hear the conversation that would develop between this pair of interlocutors. It promised to be the encounter of Thalestris and Alexander or the Queen of Sheba and Solomon. First Madame de Staël tried to overwhelm Bonaparte with an excess of compliments, which the General received in a polite but chilly manner. Another person would have gone no further, but Madame de Staël ignored the symptoms of latent hostility. Determined to have a proper conversation, she persisted by putting questions to him, all in a way to make it understood that he was the greatest of men: 'General,' she said, 'who is the woman you would like the most?' 'My wife,' he replied. 'To be sure, but who is she that you would respect the most?' 'The woman who best manages her household.' 'This too I can appreciate, but who for you would be the greatest among women?' 'The woman who produces the most children, Madame.' "

Talleyrand remained in command at the Hôtel de Galliffet until 1807, during which time he made life very difficult for Robert R. Livingston, the representative sent by the United States to negotiate the Louisiana Purchase. "You have come to a very corrupt world," is how Napoleon greeted Livingston. At that moment his mind may have been on Talleyrand, who had, we are told, "the face of a dead angel, and a fallen one at that." Talleyrand, of course, had his own opinion of himself: "I served Bonaparte when he was Emperor, just as I served him when he was Consul. I was devoted to him as long as I could believe that he was devoted to France. But when I saw him start all those revolutionary projects that spelled his ruin, I left the Ministry, and that he could not forgive." After the collapse in 1814, Napoleon had to look on from the wings as Talleyrand became the mastermind of the Congress of Vienna.

After 1814 the heirs of the Marquis de Galliffet regained possession of their family mansion. Thus, in 1821, the Foreign Ministry moved to the Rue des Capucines. Now the Hôtel de Galliffet was divided up into apartments, housing the likes of Spain's Don Francisco de Paule and the Papal nuncio. In 1894 the Italian Embassy took over the entire house and remained there until 1938, when it moved to the Hôtel de Boisgelin. Today the Hôtel de Galliffet serves as headquarters for the Italian Cultural Institute and for the Italian delegate to the Organization for Economic Cooperation and Development (OECD).

Germaine Necker, Madame de Staël
(1766–1817)

overleaf: At the Hôtel de Galliffet three large bays open to connect the vestibule with the main salon, a relationship in which the flow of space is abetted by the continuity of the structural theme of classical columns and massive entablatures. A subtle distinction is made, however, by means of the Ionic order used in the vestibule and the Corinthian order in the salon. Originally, mirrors covered all the panels, both on the walls and on the doors. In the 19th century the salon lost its reflecting revetments, which were replaced by imitation Louis XV relief decorations. By repeating every perspective into infinity, the mirrors in the salon would have joined those in the vestibule to create the effect of a vast hypostyle hall, a veritable forest of columns. The ceiling decorated in Greco-Roman motifs completes the evocation of the antique world.

Hôtel Matignon

Since 1934 the official residence of the Premier of France, the Hôtel Matignon was a product of the Régence period and played an important role in the development of the Rococo style. The mansion was designed in 1722 by Jean Courtonne, but much of its princely decoration must be attributed to Nicolas Pineau and Louis Herpin who prepared the way for the achievements of Boffrand in the Hôtel de Soubise. And, here again, the name borne by the house has nothing to do with either the designer or his patron, who in this instance was Christian-Louis de Montmorency, Prince de Tingry. Like his father, the Duc de Luxembourg so valued as a general by Louis XIV, the Prince de Tingry had a brilliant military career and became a marshal of France. Indeed he was known to the Parisian public as the "banner-maker of Notre-Dame," for the ranks of enemy standards that hung in the cathedral's great nave, all trophies taken in battles won by the Prince-Maréchal de Tingry. Still, this grandee could be eccentric. To build the so-called Hôtel Matignon, he acquired an older town house and set about to clear the land for fresh construction. But then he sold the new hôtel just short of its actual completion, conveying the property in 1723 to Jacques III Goyon, Comte de Matignon, governor of Cherbourg, Granville, and Saint-Lô.

As might be expected, the circumstance of this acquisition by the Comte de Matignon are known from the diaries of the Duc de Saint-Simon, who spent his days, and most nights, wandering through the forest of France's great family trees, ever eager to cut down and prune away the pretensions of each and every upstart. According to Saint-Simon, the Comte de Matignon acquired the Tingry house in consequence of his having lost another, to which he was entitled for every reason except the letter of the law. In 1708, Matignon had assumed the guardianship of the two minor sons of the recently deceased Comte de Marsan, whose

Talleyrand (1754–1838)

The Hôtel Matignon was built in 1720–25 from designs by Jean Courtonne. The two main façades are quite similar, both balanced, equilateral compositions accented at the center with a three-sided, projecting bay. On the garden side **(top)**, the bay is pedimented and quoined; on the courtyard side **(opposite)** it is decorated with sculptural trophies and keystones and concluded at the summit with a simple balustrade, where formerly two figures supported an armorial shield.

wife was the sister of Madame de Matignon. (To complicate matters further, the two women were also the daughters of the Comte de Matignon's elder brother!) In entrusting his sons to Matignon, the Comte de Marsan had also granted "the broadest authority and the fullest confidence." And "everyone acknowledged," so said Saint-Simon, "that the Comte de Matignon fulfilled his task with all the care, attention, and tenderness of a true father and with the success of an able man of great probity." Finding the Marsan estate heavily encumbered with debt, Matignon decided to sell the Hôtel de Marsan and with the proceeds to satisfy the most pressing of the creditors. And in the course of exercising his power in this matter, he also came to believe that he had the power to purchase the house for himself, despite his position as guardian of the property's minor heirs. This irregularity made the well-meaning Comte de Matignon vulnerable, and so when the elder Marsan son—the Prince de Pons—reached maturity and married (Mademoiselle de Roquelaure), he immediately "asked the Duc d'Elboeuf to go to Matignon and say that he [the former ward] felt obliged to claim the Hôtel de Matignon, which was the Hôtel de Marsan that the Comte de Matignon had bought and paid for. At the same time, [the Prince de Pons] did not wish the Comte de Matignon ever to dream of moving out; indeed he wanted him to remain there for the rest of his life. Surprised and indignant, Matignon replied curtly that he had good reason not to fear eviction, and while thanking [young Pons] for his courtesy, he also asserted that he did not have to accept a pretended kindness. Furthermore, should he lose the house through due process, he would leave the premises forthwith and never again set foot thereupon. And when the Prince de Pons brought action, he also brought universal approbrium upon himself. Matignon chose to be sued, for all was in his favor—save the letter of the law. Thus he lost, solely because of the guardianship that had been imposed upon him, all of which was deplored by both public and judges. The day of the ruling, Matignon moved in with his brother and set about to purchase and virtually to rebuild the superb mansion that his own son now occupies and that he has so splendidly enlarged and decorated."

The master genealogist Saint-Simon further informs us that in 1715 the Comte de Matignon married his son to Louise-Hyppolite Grimaldi, heiress of the Prince de Monaco, Duc de Valentinois. "The Prince had only daughters and no hope of having other children. His affairs were entangled, and he frankly sought a way out by bartering away his dignity through his eldest daughter. . . . What he needed was a man of quality willing, for the benefit of himself and his posterity, to give up forever his name, arms, and liveries and to assume those of the Grimaldis. Naturally, he should also be rich enough to contribute money to the Prince himself, to provide dowries for the two younger daughters, and moreover to pay off the host of creditors now laying siege to Monaco. As if this were not sufficient, the Grimaldi connection would require a cash payment and an ample annuity for the Abbé de Monaco, the Prince's brother, who would insist upon these benefits before ceding any of his rights. . . . But Matignon had the means to satisfy all the grandiose demands. In exchange for his largesse, the Comte de Matignon obtained for his son the title of Prince de Monaco and, even more important at this time, that of the Duc de Valentinois, which should normally have lapsed with the old Prince, but which, by favor of the King [Louis XIV in the final year of his life], was revived." The Grimaldi dynasty that now ensued is the one into which Grace Kelly of Philadelphia married in 1956.

In 1804 the reigning Prince de Monaco sold the Hôtel Matignon to a Mrs. Sullivan, whose beauty brought her a great career as an adventuress. Born in 1750, Anna Eleanora Franchi, the daughter of a Lucch-

The grand interior hall at the Hôtel Matignon is paved in an abstract design of colored marbles.
The basin at the center was copied after an Italian Baroque prototype now at the Château de Champs.

At the Hôtel Matignon this salon is paneled in superb cream-and-gilt *boiseries* dating probably from 1725–30.

ese tailor, had begun life as a dancer married to a dancer. Soon she engaged the affections of the Duke of Württemberg, who took his beloved to Stuttgart and set her up as the Countess of Franquemont. From this attachment came two children, both of whom the Duke legitimatized. (One of these became the mother of the celebrated dandy Comte d'Orsay, whose family name now graces the *quai* on the left bank of the Seine near the Hôtel Matignon.) Tiring of Stuttgart, the ballerina moved on to Vienna, where she readily seduced Joseph II. Soon, Paris called, and there she met an Englishman named Sullivan, who took her to India as his wife. Now Mrs. Sullivan struck up with Quentin Crawford, a wealthy Scotsman doubling as a secret agent. Leaving India for France, the couple entered the circle of the Swedish Count Fersen, Marie-Antoinette's favorite. Thus, it was at the Hôtel Matignon that Mrs. Sullivan and Crawford hid the great carriage that was to take the royal family out of Revolutionary France in 1791, only to be arrested at Varennes. At the mansion Mrs. Sullivan gave one brilliant, cosmopolitan reception after another before selling the house in 1808 to the Duc de Talleyrand, then Europe's wiliest diplomat. The new owner enlarged the hôtel once again, adding a banqueting hall as well as a concert hall, and there, on orders from Napoleon, gave a dinner four times a week for thirty-six notables—ministers, justices, senators, deputies—for the purpose of keeping the Emperor informed of all opinions current among his official appointees.

In 1840 the Simmons Bank in Brussels failed, causing the Prince of Benevento (as Napoleon styled Talleyrand) a million and a half in gold francs. In these circumstances, he was more than happy to sell the Hôtel Matignon to the Emperor, who made no use of it whatever. Under the Restoration, Louis XVIII gave the house, in exchange for the Palais de l'Élysée, to the Duchesse de Bourbon, who on her death left the property to Madame Adélaïde, her niece and the daughter of the future Louis-Philippe. Madame Adélaïde lived there until 1830, when she let the property to an American, Colonel Thorp.

The Duc de Montpensier, as the nephew of Madame Adélaïde, inherited the Hôtel Matignon and in 1848, from July to December, let it to General Cavaignac, the former governor of Algeria who helped control the rioting masses during the revolution of that year, and who, in the presidential election that followed, would be resoundingly defeated by Louis-Napoleon. In 1852 the Duc de Montpensier sold the house to the Duke of Galliera, an enormously rich financier from Genoa. The Duchess of Galliera, a relation of the Princesse de Monaco, gave magnificent receptions at the Hôtel Matignon, attracting there the cream of political and literary Paris in the time of the Second Empire. In 1877, after the fall of Napoleon III, the widowed Duchess placed the ground floor of her house at the disposal of the Comte de Paris, Louis-Philippe's grandson and the pretender to the French throne. It was there in 1886 that the betrothal of the Princesse Marie-Amélie d'Orléans to Prince Charles of Portugal proved so sumptuous and drew so much popular attention that it seemed a proclamation of the pretender's rights. The occasion merely hastened the decision, long deliberated by the Republic, to pass the Law of Exile, forbidding the heads of families that had held the throne of France from ever residing on French soil. Evidently offended, the Duchess left her vast art collection to the city of Genoa, after she had already built a museum to house it in Paris. With a fine sense of irony, she willed the empty structure to the city of Paris, but left the Hôtel Matignon to Emperor Franz-Joseph of Austria-Hungary, who there installed his embassy. Confiscated in 1919 as enemy property, the house was used for a variety of purposes until 1934, when it became the official residence of the Premier of France.

The sitting room at the Hôtel Matignon **(opposite)** fills the house's central pavilion on the garden side. The paneling is in the finest Rococo style, while the overdoor cartouches are filled with monochrome blue *chinoiserie* scenes, executed in the manner of Huet. No less fine is the paneling in the corresponding room upstairs **(above),** where the overdoors and tondo paintings have been attributed to the school of Boucher.

Hôtel du Châtelet

The classicism of ancient Greece and Rome had provided the stylistic vocabulary of French architecture since the arrival of the Renaissance in the 16th century. And by the second half of the 17th century, in the reign of Louis XIV, the architects of France had achieved a formulation of classicism that was distinctively and enduringly French. Then, quite miraculously, toward the end of Louis XV's reign, in the third quarter of the 18th century, this long-lived and fertile tradition, just before it began to burn out in decadence, received a fresh and startling new impetus. This came from the archaeological finds at Herculaneum and Pompeii, as well as from the whole mood of moral regeneration—actually a Romantic mood leading to the Revolution—that seemed to find its most expressive symbol in the cultural forms of Greco-Roman antiquity. In Paris, the Hôtel du Châtelet, built in 1770–71 from plans by Mathurin Cherpitel, was one of the first private residences to give effect to the new trend—Neoclassicism. Now, for the sake of a noble, almost severe purity of environment, the forms of architecture—columns, pilasters, entablatures, cornices, pediments, and niches—would be taken inside and used as decorative themes for interiors, both on their structural surfaces and in their furnishings.

Cherpitel's patron was the Comte du Châtelet. This member of the Lorraine's old feudal nobility achieved a distinguished career in his own right, but he enters history more frequently as the son of Émilie de Breteuil, Marquise du Châtelet, who was a notable mathematician and physicist and the lover of Voltaire. It was during the poet's stay at the Berlin court of Frederick II in 1743 that Madame du Châtelet made her home in Paris' Hôtel Lambert.

The Comte du Châtelet possessed none of the literary and scientific tastes of his mother and Voltaire. Like his father, he was an army officer. For a short time he served as French ambassador to Venice and Vienna. Made Duke in 1772 and Lieutenant General in 1780, he represented the nobility in 1789 at the meeting of the Estates General that led to the Revolution. He did not care to emigrate and was guillotined in 1794.

After a long and highly varied career, the Hôtel du Châtelet has since 1905 been the headquarters of France's Ministry of Labor.

above: The Hôtel du Châtelet reflects both inside and out the rigorously reformed, purified, and monumentalized classicism that emerged in the last years of Louis XV's reign and became dominant throughout the eras of Louis XVI, the Revolution, the Consulate, the Directory, the Empire, and the Restoration, spanning from the late 1760s to the 1820s. While the origins of Neoclassicism can be found in the "Vitruvian" architecture of Jacques-Ange Gabriel, especially in the Petit Trianon at Versailles and in Paris' École Militaire and Place de la Concorde, it took on its most powerful expression in the more "Platonic," or abstract, work of Claude-Nicolas Ledoux, whose Louveciennes pavilion for Madame du Barry was almost exactly contemporary with the Hôtel du Châtelet. Built in 1770–77, the Châtelet mansion presents on its main façade a projecting central bay, or portico, styled like a colossal Corinthian colonnade of engaged elements surmounted by a simple entablature and balustrade. The attic story—mansarded at either end and crowned by vases at the center—helps to emphasize the harmonious centrality and balance of the composition, which includes low lateral wings. There the arcade concept is continuous with the ground floor of the main *corps de logis.*

opposite: No less "architectural" is the foyer, an interior space invaded by the stone material and the structural vocabulary of the classical exterior. The stairs' handrail, with its flattened, openwork balusters and gilding, is the work of a master ironsmith.

opposite: The décor of the main sitting room in the Hôtel du Châtelet—restrained, noble, given to straight rather than curved lines, and Pompeiian instead of Rococo in its embellishments—is fully consonant with the Neoclassical mood of rigor and reform. A design preserved in the Stockholm Museum gives evidence of how the furniture in this room was originally disposed. Except for a console table under a wall mirror, the space contained only seats. Two sofas were aligned on either side of the fireplace, and a third in front of the console table. An outer circle of twenty armchairs was arranged against walls, windows, and blind doors. At the center of the room appeared another set of chairs, sixteen in all, ordered in an oval broken by the axis from entrance portals to fireplace. While the centralized composition in the sitting room was demanded by the space's "cut-off" corners, that in the dining room **(below)** springs from the cornerless oval shape of the overall space. Here the Ionic order has replaced the Corinthian, enriched by swags of garlands and marble wall fountains, in which gilded dolphins splash at the base of monumental urns *à l'antique.*

126

Hôtel de Boisgelin

Since its construction in 1732–33, the elegantly proportioned façades and salons of the Hôtel de Boisgelin have witnessed and borne the impress of many lives, all experienced with the compelling sense of self-importance that makes life go forward with spirit and energy. Here indeed is evidence of what more than one generation assumed to be the last word in taste and refinement. John Ruskin might well have had in mind the Hôtel de Boisgelin when he spoke of "the golden stain of time," for people have *lived* in this great mansion and much remains to tell us what they approved of.

Properly enough, the hôtel has acquired the name of the most memorable of its 18th-century occupants, Ramond de Boisgelin, who was Archbishop of Aix and one of the great freethinkers in an age when such activity led inexorably to the Revolution of 1789–94. Before his

At the Hôtel de Boisgelin the elevation on the garden side **(below)** and on the courtyard side **(opposite)** was radically modified in 1875–80. The original building, erected in 1732–33 from plans by Jean-Sylvain Cartaud, consisted on the garden of a two-story, seven-bay main building, covered by a dormered Mansart roof and flanked by two small pavilions of one story each. The remodeling carried out in the 19th century raised the height of the upper story and extended it over the low, lateral pavilions. At the same time, the roof was modified and partially concealed by a balustrade, and the balconies were added. A terrace leads to the garden.

arrival in the Rue de Varenne, however, the house was built for a certain Gérard Heusch, who served as Louis XV's private secretary. The plans came from Jean-Sylvain Cartaud, an architect favored by the great banker Maecenas Antoine Crozat. By 1782 the property belonged to Archbishop Boisgelin, whose powers as an orator transcended his leftest convictions to make him the preacher at most of the age's important royal funerals, including those of the Dauphin; his father, Louis XV; and the latter's son-in-law, Stanislas Leczinski, the deposed King of Poland who became Duc de Lorraine. For his radical thought, Boisgelin enjoyed the high esteem of the like-minded *philosophes*—the great men of the French Enlightenment—and no wonder. He had the temerity, when preaching at the coronation of Louis XVI in 1775, to remind the new monarch— the most modest and unvoluptuous man to occupy the French throne since Saint Louis himself—that he would do well to beware of the luxury and loose living of his predecessors. While this scandalized the court, it gave enormous delight to the advocates of reform, whose numbers were now growing apace. The orator's daring bit of liberalism did much to gain him a seat in the French Academy the following year. Yet he was no prisoner of the left, for he openly professed to "despise anarchy just as much as despotism." A deputy for the clergy at the Estates General in 1789, he voted for the abolition of privilege and for an annual tax assessment, but attempted to resist the Civil Constitution of the Clergy and the confiscation of Church property. Unintimidated by the gathering violence, Boisgelin remained in his Paris town house until 1792, when a "constitutional" Bishop was nominated for the archdiocese of Aix. And when he left for England it was under the protection of an official passport. Boisgelin returned to France in 1802 as Archbishop of Tours, and in 1804 he received the Cardinal's hat.

Boisgelin's decision to join the émigrés resulted in the immediate seizure of his property. The hôtel was then sold in 1807 to Comte Bigot de Préameneu, an author of the *code civile* and the minister of religious affairs under the Empire. In 1837 his heirs sold the house to the Comte de Bourbon-Conti, whose wife in her second marraige conveyed it in 1841 to the Duc de Doudeauville, the bearer of a name that would be identified with the Hôtel de Boisgelin for almost a century.

Sosthène de La Rochefoucauld, Duc de Doudeaville, has been described as one of the most complacent men in the complacent epoch of the Orleanist King, Louis-Philippe. "I have nothing to fear," Louis-Philippe announced in 1848, a year in which revolution swept across monarchical Europe like contagion, even causing Queen Victoria, the occupant of the world's most secure throne, to go into seclusion on the Isle of Wight, while the Duke of Wellington took the precaution of deploying troops in Westminster. But as dawn rose on this fateful year, the eighteenth in the reign of Louis-Philippe, the "Citizen King" declared: "I am necessary," content to have the keynote of his era sounded by Prime Minister Guizot: *Enrichissez-vous! Enrichissez-vous!* This the bourgeoisie did with growing appetite, all the while heedless of the misery into which

left: The glory of the Hôtel de Boisgelin is its grand staircase, built about 1875 by the architect Parent after the great 17th-century polychrome, marble-veneered models at Versailles. The tapestries on the walls were woven at the Gobelins from designs by Jean-François de Troy (1679–1752). They depict the story of Esther. Tradition holds that these works were a gift from Louis XV to the Emperor of China. The Duc de Doudeauville acquired them following the sack of the Summer Palace in Peking in 1886.
opposite: The Chinese Room was installed after the Hôtel de Boisgelin came into the possession of the Italian Embassy. Entirely European in execution, the wall panels were painted in the Oriental style of the 18th century and come from a castle in the Piedmont of northern Italy. The furniture was made in Venice during the same period.

pages 134–135: The décor of the theatre and the dining rooms is now quite thoroughly and exuberantly Italian. Designed in the 18th-century style by Adolfo Loewi just before World War II, it incorporates some priceless period elements. In the dining room, the four paintings on the walls and that on the ceiling are by Francesco Guardi and come from the Palazzo Mocenigo in Venice. The woodwork in the theatre originally adorned a palace in Palermo.

below: The large central salon is the only interior at the Hôtel de Boisgelin that retains its original paneling, carved in a delicate Rococo style and featuring "cascades" of trophies. In the 19th century the mirror opposite the one shown here was replaced by plate glass, which opened a view into the adjacent morning room **(opposite)**. The perspective effect that resulted is captivating, but quite alien to the spirit of intimacy cultivated in the 18th century.

the lower classes had been driven by the displacements of the Industrial Revolution.

In his own right, Sostène de La Rochefoucauld proved to be the perfect exemplum of the reactionary forces that took command of France in the aftermath of the Revolution. His most historic acts, after being named minister of fine arts under Charles X, the last of the Bourbons, were to require that fig leaves be added to cover the heroic nudity of the Louvre's classical statuary and that ballerinas at the Opéra dance in longer skirts. No less unfortunate was the role played by the Duc de Doudeauville in politics. Enamored of Madame du Cayla, the mistress of Louis XVIII in his infirm and lonely old age, Doudeauville moved with her behind the scenes to promote the appointment of Joseph, Comte de Villèle, as Louis XVIII's prime minister in 1822. This incredible man had his single greatest moment when he caused a bill to be passed allowing the émigrés to be reimbursed for their losses in the Revolution. The cost of the compensation came to a thousand million francs! To foot this bill, the crown reduced the rate of interest paid on government bonds from 5 to 3 percent, which discomfited the bourgeoisie, who, as they had done in 1789, took revenge by fostering a revolt against the Bourbons.

In 1876 Doudeauville's son by his first marriage—Marie-Charles-Gabriel-Sosthène de La Rochefoucauld, Duc de Bisaccia and Duc de Doudeauville—purchased the Hôtel de Boisgelin. Along with the house, he also received the conservative values that had long prevailed there. All the while he served in the National Assembly as deputy for the Sarthe and in London as French ambassador, he never ceased to dream of a restoration of the senior line of the Bourbon dynasty, the living representative of which was the Comte de Chambord. In 1873, following the collapse of Napoleon III and the Communard tyranny in Paris, Doudeauville resigned his diplomatic post in order to promote a bill making possible the accession of Chambord as Henri V. Unfortunately, the grandson of Charles X was "honor-mad," and not even for the sake of a popular restoration would he accept the crown as long as the flag of France remained the *tricolore* of the Revolution rather than the *fleur-de-lis* of royal France. Thus, it was in the anguish of his disappointment that Doudeauville consoled himself by rehabilitating the Hôtel de Boisgelin. After raising the height of the upper main story, he installed a beautiful set of *boiseries* salvaged from the dismantled Château de Bercy. Perhaps inspired by the glory of a grand staircase built in the hôtel in 1875 and modeled after the great polychrome marble ramps at Versailles, he bought a suite of Gobelins tapestries depicting the story of Esther. These had been done after the sketches of Jean-François de Troy and supposedly presented to the Emperor of China by Louis XV. Doudeauville was able to acquire them after the pillaging in 1886 of the summer palace at Peking.

Other changes were made before the Italian Embassy took over the hôtel in 1938. The theatre and the dining room were redecorated in the 18th-century Venetian manner by the architect Adolfo Loewi.

Eugène de Beauharnais (1781–1824),
Duke of Leuchtenberg

Hortense de Beauharnais (1783–1837),
Queen of Holland

Hôtel de Beauharnais

above: About 1804–05 the hôtel built in 1713 by Boffrand was given this spectacular portico, inspired by Napoleon's campaign in Egypt. **opposite:** The décor of the music room is in the manner of Prud'hon and Girodet working with Pompeiian and Assyrian motifs.

There are other miracles to be discovered in Paris, but those at the Hôtel de Beauharnais are not likely to be surpassed in the judgment of anyone excited by dazzling décor and furnishings in the Empire style. The yet unidentified artists working here in 1803–04 produced something even beyond the imagination of Percier and Fontaine, who certainly did not want for inspiration in their redesign of the Château de Malmaison for the Empress Joséphine. The Egyptian portico by an unknown architect is the perfect invitation to the wonders inside.

The house goes back to 1713 when Germain Boffrand laid it out, perhaps for his own use, and then sold the property to the Marquis de Torcy, nephew of Louis XIV's great minister Colbert and son-in-law of the Marquis de Pomponne, whom Torcy was to replace as minister of foreign affairs. In 1721, after serving six years on the Regency council, Torcy retired from public life, living on until 1746. Twenty years later the mansion was acquired by the Duc de Villeroy, who went to the scaffold in 1794 at the height of the Reign of Terror. Confiscated and then sold by the Revolutionary government, his hôtel was bought by two mean operators who broke it up into apartments. The place had fallen into a shabby state when Eugène de Beauharnais, Napoleon's stepson, took possession in 1803. Campaigning all over Europe with the Napoleonic armies and earning the title of Viceroy of Italy, Prince Eugène occupied it only briefly, in 1811 and 1812.

In the ambience of the meteoric Napoleon, everything had to move with alacrity, and so on March 22, 1804, Eugène gave a ball to inaugurate his new house, even though it was far from completed and the only place fit for guests was the ground-floor gallery. By New Year's Day, 1806, however, his sister Hortense (Queen of Holland and the mother of the future Napoleon III) could describe to Eugène the *fête* she had given in

his now-finished palace: "Your house is delightful, the most beautiful and the smartest in Paris. Even the apartment downstairs, which is the least attractive, was admired by everyone."

Despite his preoccupations abroad, Eugène had set his architects' mind on fire, a feat that was not appreciated by the Emperor: "My son, you have made a muddle of your affairs in Paris," Napoleon wrote him on February 3, 1806. "I have been handed a bill of one and a half million francs for your house. This is a huge sum." What were Eugène's steward and the various artists but a set of rascals? "I can see," continued Napoleon, "that they have mixed up everything so artfully that it will be impossible to get off without paying a great deal. I am sorry about this, for I thought you were more prudent. No work should ever be undertaken without an estimate, and a commitment not to exceed it." Eugène, who had just married Princess Amelia Augusta of Bavaria, was most embarrassed and wrote back on February 12, doing his best to defend himself.

In 1814, after Napoleon's fall, the Hôtel de Beauharnais was requisitioned by the Allies to serve as the Paris residence of Frederick William III, King of Prussia, who, having developed a taste for it, bought the house from Prince Eugène, now styled as the Duke of Leuchtenberg, and turned it into the Prussian legation. Thus, in 1862, there came to the mansion the most important man ever to live at this address—Otto van Bismarck-Schönhausen, who for six months was Prussian ambassador to Paris, just before being named Prime Minister. He wrote to his wife: "The Quai d'Orsay is a street that runs between the Seine and our garden. The garden is ten feet higher than the street. From there, through a screen of bushes, we can see the river below, and beyond that the mass of trees in the Tuileries Gardens. . . . The scene could make us forget that we live at the center of Paris. With four hundred feet of woods spread out at the foot of the lawn, one could be in the country."

In 1867 Bismarck returned to the Hôtel de Beauharnais in the company of William I, who came to Paris to gaze at the World's Fair and to entertain Napoleon III and Eugénie. "Everything went off wonderfully," commented one of the embassy secretaries when the ball for the Emperor and Empress of France was over one June 12. "In the garden we had erected a kind of gallery for supper. Flowers were in great profusion everywhere. The reception rooms, all put quite new, looked superb. The garden, which was meant to play a major role in the occasion, was tastefully lighted. At ten o'clock the company began to arrive, followed by the court at eleven. The King received them downstairs and accompanied the Empress Eugénie upstairs. A crowd gathered wherever the sovereigns were. Dancing lasted until half-past midnight, when Their Majesties took supper in the garden's temporary gallery. . . . A cotillon followed at two. . . . Everything went splendidly. The King and his imperial guests lingered long and enjoyed watching the dancers. . . . One of the most successful features of the evening was the barrel of beer set up in the garden. Count von Bismarck stopped there for a long while . . . ."

The decent, but far from brilliant, William would be puzzled again and again by the Bismarck diplomacy that led from war to war until, on January 18, 1871, he was crowned Emperor of Germany in the Hall of Mirrors at Versailles. For the modest bearer of this arrogant crown, the coronation constituted "the most dreadful day of my life."

Although the present chancery building of the Federal Republic of Germany is a rather dull modern affair on the Right Bank, the Hôtel de Beauharnais has been meticulously restored to serve as the official residence of the West German ambassador. And if possible, the ensemble commissioned by Prince Eugène seems even more spectacular than ever.

The boudoir at the Hôtel de Beauharnais is decorated in an Empire reinterpretation of the fanciful, pseudo-Turkish style that had gained popularity in 18th-century France.

above: In the bedroom of Queen Hortense at the Hôtel de Beauharnais, the mahogany bed with its high canopy supported by four columns must, like the gilded swan-neck armchairs, be counted among the finest examples of furnishings that survive from the period of the early 19th-century Empire.   **opposite:** In the bathroom of Queen Hortense the walls lined with mirrors endlessly multiply the tall, slender marble colonettes and the ceiling panels painted in the Pompeiian manner.   **pages 42–43:** For all its gilt and crystal, the Salon of the Seasons at the Hôtel de Beauharnais is lavish without excess. Thus, it marks a transition from the style of the Directory to the weighty and grandiose, but essentially severe and straight-line, manner of the Empire. The two large paintings are attributed to the school of Prud'hon.

Hôtel de Roquelaure

top: Save for the central flight of steps, the exterior of the Hôtel de Roquelaure has not been altered since its construction. **above and opposite:** The vestibule is decorated with reliefs, superbly designed and carved in stone.

Everyone loves a survivor, but some survivors inspire less rejoicing than others. One rather ominous survivor of the Revolution was Jean-Jacques de Cambacérès, Duke of Parma and arch-chancellor of the Empire, who from 1808 to 1814 made his home in the superb setting of the Hôtel de Roquelaure. A member of the Convention who voted for the death of Louis XVI, Cambacérès was suspected of knowing entirely too much about the unauthorized disappearance of the son of Louis XVI and Marie-Antoinette. But for the very reason of his all-embracing knowledge of an era fraught with complications, Napoleon decided that Cambacérès could be useful.

The scion of a noted judicial family in Montpellier, Cambacérès found himself in charge of the tribunal of the Hérault *département* when the Revolution broke out in 1789. By the time of the Terror his distinctive qualities had caused him to be chosen president of the Committee of Public Safety, whose grim responsibility was to select those to be sent to the guillotine. "He had the very best of relations with all the parties that dominated the Convention [the body that governed Revolutionary France from 1792 to 1795]," declared one of his shrewder colleagues. "Ever calm, always the master of his emotions, he always made his first concern his own safety, his second for any part he might play." But for all his caution, he did hazard a strong personal opinion when people began to speak of sending the royal children out of the country. "We shan't run any danger if we keep the members of the Capet family in prison," he argued. "And we could get into trouble by sending them into exile. If Rome had kept the Tarquins prisoners, Rome would not have had to contend with them. Just imagine," Cambacérès pointed out, "that the heir of the Capets is there in the midst of our enemies. In no time you'll find out that he'll be on hand at every point where our legions are

striking down our enemies. Even after he has departed this life, he'll be thought of everywhere, and this absurdity will inflame the guilty hopes of all Frenchman who are traitors to their country." When Louis XVII did disappear, there were those who whispered: "Cambacérès alone could tell us what happened to the little Prince. No one else can solve that riddle."

As Arch-Chancellor of the Empire, Cambacérès had the right to be addressed as Your Most Serene Highness. Napoleon soon regretted this, realizing there was too much of a muchness about it. But in this office as everywhere else, Cambacérès took his dignity very seriously. "In public, call me Most Serene Highness," he once reminded his private secretary. "But between ourselves you need only call me *monseigneur*." Such hauteur demanded the most tedious etiquette, and this in turn spoiled the otherwise splendid social events staged by Cambacérès at the Hôtel de Roquelaure. According to the Duchesse d'Abrantès, dinner was served at six, and from seven on the guests had to file by to pay their court to

The interior of the Hôtel de Roquelaure was decorated in 1733 from designs prepared, not by Lassurance, who had died in 1724, but by Le Roux. The *boiseries* illustrated here from the small salon are exuberantly Rococo in the Louis XV manner, but nonetheless discreet and orderly.

the host. But since no guest was allotted more than a quarter of an hour, by half-past eight the house was empty and Cambacérès free to set out for the theatre.

The arch-chancellor could also be curt with women, as Madame de La Rochefoucauld, Empress Joséphine's lady-in-waiting, was well aware. "What a charming negligé you're wearing," he told her when she appeared too informally dressed for his taste. "Please excuse me," Madame de La Rochefoucauld answered, "I have just come from calling on the Empress and have not had the time to change my clothes." This lack of gallantry reflected a predilection that even Napoleon knew about. Once when Cambacérès turned up a quarter of an hour late for an appointment stammering, "Excuse me, Sire, the fact is that I was with a lady," the Emperor glared and snapped: "The next time you find yourself with a lady and see the hour approaching when you have an appointment with the Emperor, you can tell her to take her cane and hat and be off!"

The Hôtel de Roquelaure deserved better, for from the outset it was one of the truly memorable monuments of the Rococo style. Pierre Cail-

146

letaux, known as Lassurance, undertook the house in 1722 under commission from two speculators who sold it in 1726 to the Duc de Roquelaure. The building has been completed by Jean-Baptiste Le Roux afte Lassurance died in 1724. Then it was not until 1733 that the interior décor with all its delicate intricacy could be completed.

As the inimitable Saint-Simon put it, Gaston-Jean-Baptiste-Antoine de Roquelaure was "everyone's friend and trusted by no one." Yet his manners were agreeable, and he could now and then toss off a witty remark, even at his own expense. The Duchesse de Roquelaure, *née* Marie-Louise de Montmorency-Laval, had attracted the attention of the ever-susceptible Louis XIV, and her first child, a daughter, came into this world quite soon after her hasty marriage. "Welcome, young lady," the Duke is supposed to have said, "I did not expect you so soon."

Years later this young lady made a runaway match with the Prince de Léon, son of the Duc de Rohan. The Rohan and Roquelaure families had at first agreed on the marriage, but, so Saint-Simon tells us, "when they came to sign the contract, they could only exchange harsh words, thanks to the arrogance of the Duchesse de Roquelaure, who was anxious to extract more money from the Duc de Rohan." If the Rohans were vulnerable, it was because of the unpromising qualities of their young man. The Prince de Léon was a tall lean fellow, and as ugly as anyone could imagine. Still, he had wit and wile and could not have been more at home in the great world. As for Mademoiselle de Roquelaure, she may have thought herself well matched in the Rohan boy. Also ugly, she was moreover a hunchback. And she too could think for herself, possessed as she was of a bold, resolute, and enterprising mind.

The possibility that their marriage might be called off plunged the two lovers into despair. The Prince de Léon feared his father might maneuver him into some other marriage requiring even less money. And Mademoiselle de Roquelaure fancied that her mother, out of avarice, might not let her marry at all, but rather send her off to some convent. So Léon and his fiancée eloped, arranging for a wedding to be held in a small house in Ménilmontant belonging to Saint-Simon's brother-in-law.

Outraged, the Duchesse de Roquelaure headed straight for Marly to seek redress from Louis XIV himself. The news spread rapidly, and she received her meed of pity. But then the whole court fell to laughing at the ludicrous abduction of this hunchbacked girl by so ungainly a suitor. Finally order was restored, although both families were so resentful that they cut down on the settlements.

Poverty prevented either the Princesse de Léon or her sister, the Princesse de Pons (whose husband had made a spurious but nonetheless successful claim to the original Hôtel Matignon [see page 118]), from ever enjoying the Hôtel de Roquelaure, for the two daughters found it necessary to sell the house just as soon as their father had died. The new owner was Mathieu-François Molé, the descendant of an old family of the *noblesse de la robe* and son-in-law of the great banker Samuel Bernard. Molé, who had Jean-Michel Chevotet build him the glorious Château de Champlatreux in the Île-de-France, could not fail to appreciate the subtle art of Lassurance and Le Roux. During the Revolution Molé, at age ninety-two, perished on the scaffold, as did his son, and in 1793 the Hôtel de Roquelaure was confiscated. Three years later it was restored to Comte Molé, who in 1808 ceded the house to Cambacérès.

In 1815 Louis XVIII acquired the hôtel in order to give it to the Duchesse d'Orléans in exchange for the Hôtel de Toulouse, which was now occupied by the Banque de France. After the Princess' death in 1821, the Roquelaure house was taken over by the Council of State. Since 1840 it has sheltered the Ministry of Public Works.

At the Hôtel de Roquelaure the *boiseries* in the grand salon are, after the 18th-century fashion, the richest and most ornate in the house. If the Ionic pilasters that structure the composition continue a tradition going back to the earliest Renaissance, the rest of the décor, with its "chicory" motifs, its laces and flower-filled vases, its "cascades" of musical instruments, conforms to the purest Rococo manner. The gilded reliefs filling the cornice corners are particularly delightful, depicting children at a variety of games.

Louis de Rouvray, Duc de Saint-Simon (1675–1755)

Hôtel de Saint-Simon

The Hôtel de Saint-Simon merits its name, for certainly the most unforgettable personage ever to live there was Louis de Rouvray, Duc de Saint-Simon, even though this avid and sharp-eyed observer of the twilight court of Louis XIV and the succeeding Regency never owned the property, but merely rented the ground-floor apartment. The house, like those on either side of it, had been erected in 1682–88 by the neighboring Dominicans as a source of income for their novitiate. Originally, the buildings had gardens on the back and, on the front, courtyards that gave into the Rue Saint-Dominique, which just here became the Boulevard Saint-Germain in the 19th century. Nothing of the décor and furnishings that surrounded Saint-Simon has survived in the hôtel where he lived from 1714 to 1746, after having moved there with his mother, his wife, his two sons, and a daughter. But mere physical reminders are hardly necessary given the vivid presence that springs from the pages of the *Mémoires* that the Duke composed—in large part if not entirely—while a lease-holder in the Rue Saint-Dominique.

No one who made a mark at court, or attempted to make one, escaped the notice of Saint-Simon or a comment by one of the most opinionated people who ever put pen to paper. The "terrible Duke" did not shy from saying precisely what he had on his mind, even in regard to the mighty Louis XIV, especially when it came to the King's several bastards who were climbing too high in the world. And when he grew tired of working up these subjects, he would turn to Jules Hardouin-Mansart, usually considered *the* architect of Versailles.

The library in the Hôtel de Saint-Simon, where the Duke wrote his *Mémoires* between 1740 and 1750, contains beautiful 18th-century furnishings but preserves nothing from the time of the famous chronicler.

The *Mémoires* of Saint-Simon constitute a peerless portrait gallery of privileged and parvenu France in the early 18th century, the work of a man who could not resist reminding posterity that his own family went back to Charlemagne. With this pride of blood, it is no wonder that the author noted again and again that more than one prominent figure had origins in the very dregs of humanity. He knew that the aristocracy was constantly threatened. "It is true," he said, "that the titles of Count and Marquis have been dragged in the dust by the crowd of nobodies and landless creatures who have stolen their way to power." Nor was he impressed by the Dukes of England. They had no rank whatever in France! Nowhere is Saint-Simon more the aristocrat than in his frequent disregard for the rules of grammar and rhetoric. He simply transcended such academic tedium and made his accounts an intensely personal and emotional apology of a grand seigneur, prevented, mainly by pride, from accepting the rise of the bourgeoisie. If he resented Louis XIV, it was because this monarch had deprived the great nobles of their hereditary powers and independence. But Saint-Simon's *Mémoires*, for all their factual and expository flaws, are remarkable documents, psychologically acute and full of brilliant characterization, and they have long been accepted as one of the authentic monuments of French literature. The reminiscences were not published until 1788, at which time they no doubt added fuel to the rising fires of revolt against all the old Duke had stood for.

On the subject of Louis XIV Saint-Simon was inexhaustible. The King, he claimed, had been "born with a mind that was worse than mediocre, but a mind capable of being improved, polished, and refined, a mind that could borrow without imitating and without being embarrassed." When the aged monarch died, he was missed only by the meanest of his valets. However, he had had his redeeming features. Louis never failed to doff his hat to any woman, no matter how low her rank. There was a difference, of course, between ranks, but still the hat was removed. And Saint-Simon was aware that he had a royal manner. There was that moment when the King came across a victorious general. "I have no time to talk to you now," he said, "but I am creating you a Duke." And Saint-Simon remembered that Louis XIV had been profoundly religious. In his last moments on earth, dwelling on his relation to God Almighty, the expiring sovereign would murmur: "In the days when I was King."

Thanks to Saint-Simon, we know exactly what Louis said to his courtiers on August 26, 1715, five days before he died. "Gentlemen," he declared, "I beg your pardon for the bad example I have set you. I must certainly thank you for the manner in which you have served me, and for your faithfulness and devotion. I am sorry that I have not done for you the things I should like to have done. But we have been living through hard times. I ask you now to give my great-grandson the same faithful service you have given me. He is a boy who will have his troubles. May you be an example to all my other subjects. Carry out the orders that my nephew will be giving you. He is going to govern the kingdom. I hope that he will acquit himself well. I also hope that you will all work together and that if one of you should stray, that you will bring him back into the fold. I feel that I am becoming sentimental, and that I am turning you in the direction of sentimentality. I beg your pardon for that. Farewell, gentlemen. I hope you will think upon me from time to time."

And thanks to Saint-Simon we know his last words to the five-year-old Louis XV: "My child," he announced, "you will be a great King. Don't follow my example in erecting too many buildings, nor imitate me in my

Marie-Gabrielle de Lorge,
Duchesse de Saint-Simon (d. 1743)

wars. On the contrary, try to keep peace with your neighbors. Render unto God that which is His due. Live up to your obligations to Him, and be sure that your subjects hold Him in honor. Follow the best possible advice. Try to comfort your people, as I, poor man, could not."

When it came to the cast at court, Saint-Simon was completely at ease with those who knew their place. One such man was Racine, who had nothing of the poet in his conversation. As for the Regent, the Duc d'Orléans, he could never pretend to the "fearful majesty" of Louis XIV—he was sunk too deep in debauchery. Furthermore, Saint-Simon could be amused by the behavior of Louis XV's mother, the Duchesse de Bourgogne, "I'll be Queen! I'll be Queen!" she cried out one day, joyful at the thought of putting down all those impudent enough to object to the foolery she employed to amuse the elderly Louis XIV. Unfortunately, this Princess and her husband did not live to reign.

The great moment in the life of Saint-Simon arrived when he was sent to Madrid in 1721 to seek the hand of the Infanta, the three-year-old daughter of Louis XIV's grandson, King Philip V, on behalf of young Louis XV. Not only was the Order of the Golden Fleece bestowed upon the Duke's elder son, but, in addition, Saint-Simon and his younger son were made Grandees of Spain, First Class. All this was accomplished in the elaborate etiquette of the Spanish court, a spectacle that the chronicler would long treasure.

Another triumphant occasion was that on which Saint-Simon witnessed the official humiliation of the royal bastards earlier legitimatized by Louis XIV. As the Regent deprived these Princes of the rights of royal status, the Duke, a member of the Regency Council, could scarcely contain himself: "Motionless, glued to my seat, my whole body rigid, filled with all that joy can impress most keenly upon the senses, quick with the most sensual agitation, with the most inordinately and unremittingly desired enjoyment, I sweated with anguish at having to bottle up my feelings, and that very anguish was a voluptuous delight such as I have never felt before or since that day of days. How true it is that the pleasures of the senses are inferior to those of the mind."

Finally, Saint-Simon approached the sublime when he sat down in his study to settle accounts with Jules Hardouin-Mansart, whom he had long despised as a toady. The architect was a handsome man, he conceded, but "came from the scum of the earth," even though he did know a thing or two about getting on in the world. Was he the nephew of the great François Mansart? Or was he his bastard? In any event, he had wormed his way into the older master's confidence and finally had become architect-in-chief to the King. The imposter knew absolutely nothing about his profession, and neither did his brother-in-law, Robert de Cotte. The two of them got all their plans and all their ideas from a draftsman named Lassurance, whom they were careful to keep locked up. Hardouin-Mansart was a coarse fellow, capable of pulling the sleeve of a Prince of the blood. Yet he knew how to manage His Majesty. The builder would go to no end of trouble to praise the monarch's artistic instincts, with the result that when a bridge he built at Moulins—a masterpiece of solidity—suddenly collapsed, the King took no notice whatever of this misadventure.

Saint-Simon had little reason to take pleasure in his children, but his marriage—to Marie-Gabrielle de Lorge—could not have given him greater satisfaction. After the death of the Duchess in 1743, he wanted her gravestone to bear witness to "her incomparable virtues, her unshakable piety, all her life so true, so simple, so constant, so uniform, so solid, so admirable, so singularly amiable, which made her the delight and the object of admiration of all who knew her." At his death Saint-Simon asked that his coffin be bound to his wife's with iron clamps. The joint sepulchre was violated during the Revolution. Well Saint-Simon might mourn his departed spouse, for her practical sense was as great as her other virtues, and without her management, the Duke's affairs took a perilous turn, forcing him to leave his large hôtel in 1746 for a more modest abode in the Rue du Cherche-Midi. Soon a further accommodation had to be made, and it was in the Rue des Saints-Pères that he died in 1755, having sadly survived both his sons.

As Church property, the hôtel was confiscated during the Revolution and sold, passing through a variety of hands until acquired in 1889 by the Société des Immeubles de France, which still owns it. Saint-Simon's apartment is today occupied by Comte Jean de Sélancy and his wife, *née* Bertier de Sauvigny.

The foyer **(above)** and the drawing room **(opposite)** once occupied by the Duc and Duchesse de Saint-Simon were redecorated by subsequent tenants in the chaste, Neoclassical manner that arose in the reign of Louis XVI. Particularly handsome in their design are the overdoor reliefs of antique incense burners. The period furnishings are of the highest quality, especially the Régence ormolu chest between the windows on the right.

Hôtel de Salm-Dyck

The treasure of the Hôtel de Salm-Dyck lies in the Empire style decorations—especially the painted ceilings—created about 1809–10 under the direction of Anne-Louis Girodet-Trioson. Girodet, as he is known to art history, was one of the most gifted pupils to develop in the atelier of the period's great master, Jacques-Louis David. And it is in the richly coloristic, glacial yet sensuous, private, and deeply cultivated art of Girodet that we can discern the almost integral relationship of those twin currents of the time—Neoclassicism and Romanticism. The hôtel this artist lent his talents to had been built in 1723, by an architect no longer known, for a certain Pierre-Henry Le Maistre. But from the outset it was rental property, tenanted in 1726 by the Duchesse de Gramont, whose daughter, the widowed Princesse de Bournonville, married the Duc de Ruffec, Saint-Simon's elder son. The seizures of the Revolution conveyed it in 1809 to the Comte de Salm-Dyck.

Now a brilliant life came to the mansion, attracted by the charms—physical as well as literary—of the Princesse de Salm-Dyck. The daughter of the superintendent of waters and forests near Nantes, Constance de Théis had became a celebrity at age eight, thanks to the publication, in the 1785 issue of the *Almanch des graces,* of her poem entitled *Le Bouton de rose* ("The Rosebud"). From then until her death in 1845, Constance continued to write, creating a body of work that, when published in 1842, filled four volumes. She had a genuine popular success with *Sapho,* a play set to music by Martini and premiered at the Théâtre Louvois on December 14, 1794. In 1802 the author separated from her first husband, and in the following year she married Joseph de Salm-Dyck, Count of the Holy Roman Empire until this entity was abolished in 1806, then Count of the French Empire, and finally Prince de Salm, courtesy of Frederick William III of Prussia. From 1809 to 1824 the Princess de Salm-Dyck kept a salon in the Rue du Bac that was crowded with celebrities. Lafayette attended, as did the actor Talma, the botanist Jussieu, the scientist Alexander von Humboldt, the composer Grétry, and the artists Houdon, Guérin, and Horace Vernet, in addition to Girodet.

None other than Stendhal, in his *Vie de Henri Brulard,* has left a portrait of the Princess from the time when he first met her in 1800, still married to a Dr. Pipelet. Stendhal had been taken to a meeting of a poetry circle

The exquisite decorations in the foyer **(above)**, the library **(opposite)**, and the grand salon were executed around 1809–10 under the supervision of Girodet, a pupil of David and one of the great masters of the Empire style. Girodet was a privileged member of the artistic and literary circle around the Princesse de Salm-Dyck. The dining room **(top)**, by contrast, has retained its 18th-century *boiseries.*

then presided over by his cousin, Pierre Daru. "The poetry they read filled me with horror. . . . It was bourgeois and flat . . . but I longingly admired the bosom of Madame Constance Pipelet, who consented to read a few lines of her own. . . . One day I must say something about her present marriage, which was preceded by a two-month sojourn, in the company of her lover, at the Prince's château. She wanted to discover whether her lover would be content with the place."

Recently classified an historic monument, the apartment of the Princesse de Salm-Dyck has now been restored by its present owner.

above and opposite: The painted decorations in the main drawing room at the Hôtel de Salm-Dyck are believed to have been planned by Girodet and executed by his pupils. But the handsome ensemble is completed by other fine works of quite different provenance. The 17th-century Gobelins tapestry, depicting the allegory of fire, is one of a series on the Four Elements. The gilt furniture by Jacob once belonged to Marshal Soult. The large vases on either side of the fireplace are in Saint Petersburg porcelain and were gifts from Czar Nicholas I to the Duc de Mortemart, when, under Charles X, he was French ambassador to Russia. The clock on the mantelpiece, a creation of Thomire, is similar to a clock, now in Paris' Musée des Arts Decoratifs, that once stood in Marie-Antoinette's bathroom in the Tuileries Palace.

Hôtel Séguier

above: At the Hôtel Séguier entrance is gained through a simple stone archway, made handsome by the crisply articulated blocks, by the modest flourish of the central cartouche, and by the consoles supporting a balustrade.
opposite: Like most of the ground-floor apartment, the library retains its original décor, a set of panels with plain but graceful moldings.

Edith Wharton, who knew the Faubourg Saint-Germain as did no other American author, was well aware of the charms of a house like the Hôtel Séguier, dating from the 17th century. The designer has a name, which can no longer be identified, but, even so, the place was remodeled quite carefully in the late 18th century to catch the spirit of the times when bas-reliefs in the classical manner were inserted to prove that one was up to date, though perhaps not splendid.

"If," Mrs. Wharton reports, "any authentic member of the Faubourg Saint-Germain has been asked what really constituted Paris society, the answer would undoubtedly have been: *There is no Paris society any longer—there is just a welter of people from heaven knows where.*" The author could not help recalling a play by Dumas *fils* in which an indignant Duchess, confronted by her husband's mistress, cries out: "Open the windows! Let everyone come in who wants to!" "In the Paris I knew," continues Mrs. Wharton, "everyone would have told me that those windows had remained wide open ever since, that *tout le monde* had long since come in, that all the old social conventions were tottery or otherwise demolished, and that the Faubourg had become as promiscuous as the Fair of Neuilly. The same thing was no doubt said a hundred years earlier, and two hundred years even, and probably something not unlike it was heard in the more exclusive salons of Babylon and Ur."

Yet, in a town house as quiet and unpretentious as this, certain traditions have been handed down. A certain confident elegance may be expected at the Hôtel Séguier, once the residence of the Marquis de Moussy, hereditary holder of the ancient office of Cup Bearer to the King of France. Early in the 19th century the mansion was acquired by Baron Antoine Séguier, the descendant of a well-known family of magistrates. He himself was a presiding judge of the Court of Appeals.

Modesty need not be overlooked in a careful survey of this most distinguished section of Paris. We must allow for an occasional sober chandelier and a group of chaste Louis XVI chairs.

When the Hôtel Séguier was redecorated in the late 18th century, the *salon de compagnie* (**above and top**) gained its overdoor stucco reliefs. The armchairs here and in the dining room (**opposite**) are from the same period, the reign of Louis XVI.

Hôtel de Salm

"To understand thoroughly the art of living," architect Robert Adam admitted at the height of his career in London, "it is necessary, perhaps, to have passed some time among the French." In the 18th century there were Kings who agreed with him. Paris seduced Christian VII of Denmark and Gustavus III of Sweden, and Prince Henry of Prussia, Frederick the Great's brother, left the French capital in 1784 with a heavy heart.

A Prince literally willing to die for Paris was Frederick of the ancient Westphalian house of Salm-Kyrburg. Arriving in 1771, aged twenty-five, he remained in Paris to the end, despite the fatal dangers presented by the Revolution. In 1782, following his marriage to a Princess of the house of Hohenzollern-Sigmaringen, he prevailed upon the architect Pierre Rousseau, who had learned a thing or two about sculptural carving while working with the great Jacques-Ange Gabriel, to create his town house or palace on the Seine embankment at 64 Rue de Lille, just across the river from the Tuileries Gardens. The project all but ruined the Salms, both of whom had received enormous fortunes. Actually, they never did finish paying the bills, and their additional dream of a château in Alsace remained merely a dream.

In the meantime, the Prince de Salm was leading an anxious existence behind the splendid arch of triumph that framed his colonnaded courtyard. Creditors came through that generous entryway all too frequently, only to leave scowling with dissatisfaction. Just the same, the Prince felt obliged to live up to the grandiose setting he had ordered for himself and to go on playing the part of the munificent host. "Many of the people here tonight think that I, too, was invited to this ball," he told one guest who commented that half of Paris had come to the party. When his situation grew desperate, the Prince thought of marrying his nephew, then dying of consumption, to the daughter of his contractor—as if the latter would accept the alliance with a titled family as sufficient payment!

But the Prince de Salm had still other delusions, one of which proved fatal. At the same time that he indulged great pride in his blood,

The facade, with its domed rotunda inspired by Rome's 2nd-century Pantheon, that Thomas Jefferson admired so much and remembered when designing his own house, Monticello.

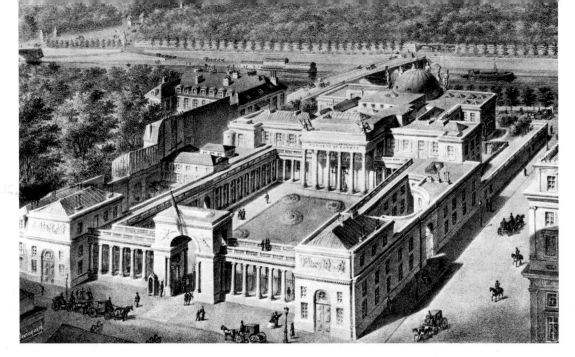

166

The Hôtel de Salm, built in 1782–87 from designs by Pierre Rousseau, is a monument to the French Neoclassical style at its purest. A great triumphal arch serves as entrance to the *cour d'honneur,* which, completely surrounded by an Ionic colonnade, evokes the atria of ancient Roman villas. On axis with the street entrance is the entrance to the palace, a great Corinthian portico supporting not a pediment but a monumentally simple entablature crowned by a blind attic. A series of bas-reliefs all in the antique style—located under the portico and on the street façades of the projecting lateral pavilions—lend a touch of animation to an otherwise severe and majestic ensemble.

he also fancied himself a man of the Enlightenment, a liberal capable of sympathy toward the Revolution. This gained him little but disrespect, even from the left, and whatever his contributions to the revolt, they did not save the Prince de Salm from the guillotine, where he was led in 1794, just across the Seine and a few steps beyond the Tuileries Gardens in the great public square now called the Place de la Concorde.

Although genealogy may be compared to a forest from which few travelers have been known to return in their right minds, a word must be said about the family of the Prince's friend, Alexandre de Beauharnais, who lost his head at the same time. Alexandre's widow, Joséphine Tascher de La Pagérie, the irresistible Creole from Martinque, survived to marry Napoleon Bonaparte, while he was still a rising young general in the French army, and thereafter to become his first Empress. And Alexandre's son Eugène—he of the Hôtel de Beauharnais—had a sister, Hortense, who married Napoleon's brother Louis and thus became Queen of Holland and the mother of the future Napoleon III. So close were the Salms and the Beauharnais that when Joséphine was arrested, the Prince de Salm's sister—Amélie, left unmolested—took charge of the two Beauharnais children, along with a nephew and an English boy. "The four of us," Hortense was to recall, "too young to understand what was going on outside, would pass the time chattering away on the great terraces of the Hôtel de Salm, as carefree and cheerful as children can be. However, when every day at a certain hour we watched the people gathering on the Place Louis XV [today the Concorde] and draw near the raised platform, which we guessed to be the site of the punishments, we went back to our rooms absolutely desolate. Tears streamed down our cheeks at the thought that those unfortunate people were dying. Little did we imagine that our own parents might have the same fate! Certain of their innocence, we waited impatiently for the hour of their deliverance."

Once the Prince was beheaded, the Hôtel de Salm's future was far from certain. Creditors had the palace handed over to his son, with the understanding that the building would be managed by an assignee in bankruptcy. The assignee then rented the hôtel to a certain Leuthereau, who had grown rich on army contracts and now styled himself Marquis de Beauregard. Taking up with Mademoiselle Lange—a notorious actress-courtesan of the era, immortalized in a satiric-allegorical portrait by Girodet—Leuthereau threw extravagant parties at the Hôtel de Salm, attended by a company far from select. After one celebration went too far even for those loose times, the operator ended up in Toulon prison, where he died in irons. But Leuthereau rented only part of the mansion, while the other part was taken over by the Constitutional Club, known as the Club de Salm, where the irrepressible Madame de Staël flirted with politicians of republican tendencies. Still later the hôtel was surrendered to the Société de Zéphyr, and balls were staged that caused the police to intervene.

In 1804 the Hôtel de Salm was purchased by the government to house the Legion of Honor, established two years before by Napoleon during his days as First Consul. The decision probably was much influenced by Joséphine's feeling for Princess Amélie. Meanwhile, Napoleon himself became the protector of the young Prince de Salm, making him a personal aide-de-camp. In 1871 the Hôtel de Salm was one of the great and symbolic buildings put to the torch by the Communards in the aftermath of another upheaval, the Franco-Prussian War. While the exterior was carefully restored to the form given it by Rousseau, the interiors, deemed beyond repair, were redone—appropriately enough—in the Empire style.

When rebuilt after 1871, the dining room in the Hôtel de Salm was designed in imitation of the great marble-encrusted staterooms at 17th-century Versailles.

above: When redecorated around 1875, the rotunda-shaped main drawing room at the Hôtel de Salm was done in a post-Second-Empire interpretation of the Louis XVI style. The clock and candelabra on the mantelpiece were gifts from the English collector and philanthropist, Sir Richard Wallace.   **opposite:** The adjacent room, the Salon des Grands Chanceliers, is hung with portraits of the Chancellors of France, all set against relief panels painted in imitation of Wedgwood china, itself an important manifestation of the Neoclassical mode. The carpet reproduces the arms of France under the Bourbon Restoration (1814–30).

Hôtel d'Avaray

In 1807, while Napoleon Bonaparte ruled as Emperor of France, the exiled Louis XVIII wrote of the Comte d'Avaray: "I owe him my life and my liberty. My obligations to him as a man are outdone by what I owe him as rightful King. I will add simply this: If only he had had another Henri IV to serve, he would have been a second Sully. . . . He gave up a fortune of 80,000 francs a year . . . to devote himself to my unhappy cause. His health has been broken down by the inroads of cruel disease, as a result of the hardships he has undergone in fifteen years as my companion in adversity, toil, and exile."

In 1791, at the height of the Revolution, Antoine-Louis-François de Bésiade, Comte d'Avaray, organized the successful escape from Paris of the Comte de Provence (Louis XVI's younger brother and the future Louis XVIII) on the night of June 20–21 (the same night on which Louis XVI and his family started on their abortive flight to Varennes). Having devotedly followed the royal Prince into exile and become his most trusted adviser, he was rewarded in 1809 with the titles of Duke and peer of the realm. Comte d'Avaray scarcely had time to enjoy the honors, for poor health obliged him to retire to Madeira, where he died in 1811.

Designed by Le Roux, the Hôtel d'Avaray was built in 1718 for Claude-Théophile de Bésiade, Marquis d'Avaray, great-grandfather of Louis XVIII's friend and follower. During the War of the Spanish Succession (1701–11) the Marquis was instrumental in gaining the French victory at Almansa (1707), for which the new Spanish King, Philip V (a French Prince and Louis XIV's grandson), made him Viceroy of Naples, then governor of the Spanish provinces of Flanders and Hainaut.

From 1724 to 1727 the Marquis d'Avaray leased his new house to the English envoy in Paris, Horatio Walpole (later Baron Walpole of Wolverton, a younger brother of Sir Robert Walpole, Prime Minister of England, and uncle of the writer Horace Walpole). The house remained in the d'Avaray family until 1920, when it was purchased by the government of The Netherlands. It now houses the Dutch Embassy.

A narrow hallway in the Hôtel d'Avaray **(above)** leads from the dining room to the grand salon **(opposite).** Here the superb trophy-decorated paneling came from an old hôtel demolished to make way for the Boulevard Raspail. It serves as a framework for the handsome 17th-century tapestries. Together, wood and weaving endow this noble space with warmth and welcome.

The Invalides

Hôtel de Biron
Hôtel de Noirmoutier
Hôtel de Besenval
Hôtel de Jarnac
Hôtel de Lassay

At the Hôtel de Lassay, the 18th-century
Salon de Musique opening into
the Second Empire Salle des Fêtes

Hôtel de Biron

The Hôtel de Biron was erected in 1728–31 for Abraham Peyrenc, a typical self-made man of his period, the heyday in France of financiers, tax farmers, and stockjobbers. Born in Languedoc in 1685, the son of a barber-wigmaker, Peyrenc came up to Paris as a teenager and found employment as a valet and hairdresser in the home of François Farges, an army contractor who had accumulated an enormous fortune. He was handsome, young Peyrenc, and it was not long before he seduced Farges' daughter. And as the budding opportunist had hoped, the promise of scandal yielded a hasty marriage. Now, with such a father-in-law, he had no difficulty landing the job of inspector general in the bank set up in Paris by the Scottish economist John Law. Here Peyrenc could make the most of the frenzied speculation in Law's schemes and discover just the right time to sell out. A true *nouveau riche*, he bought the de Moras land near the recently built Invalides and along with it acquired a title.

Soon Peyrenc de Moras decided to grace his property with "the most beautiful house Paris has ever seen," and assigned the conception of it to Jacques Gabriel, father of the creator of the Petit Trianon and the Place de la Concorde, with the work to be overseen by Jean Aubert, the architect of the main stables at Chantilly. The finished hôtel immediately became famous for the luxury of its appointments. Unfortunately, Peyrenc de Moras died in 1732, just one year after the family had moved in.

Four years later Madame Peyrenc de Moras let the hôtel to the Duchesse du Maine, whom we met at the Arsenal. Her tenure in the Rue de Varenne assured this outlying neighborhood of a brilliant social and cultural life. It was there that Voltaire wrote *Zadig*.

Now the Peyrenc de Moras family sold the property to the Duc de Biron, for whom the hôtel has been called ever since. Seriously wounded at the siege of Prague in 1741, Biron had five horses killed under him at

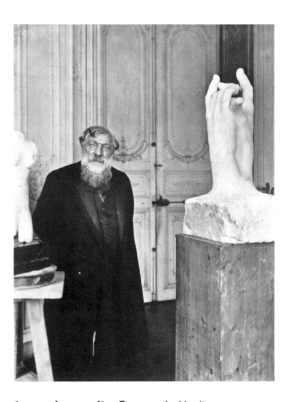

top and opposite: Surrounded by its magnificent parklike setting, the Hôtel de Biron seems more a country château than Parisian town house.
above: After it was broken up into apartments in 1902, the Hôtel de Biron became the home of the creative: Cocteau, Matisse, Isadora Duncan, Rilke, and Rodin. Rodin so identified with the house that in 1916 a law was passed making the mansion the Musée Rodin.

the Battle of Fontenoy. In 1767 he received the marshal's baton and in 1775 the governorship of Languedoc. The style of the Birons was of an elegance, even an opulence, to make that of the Duchesse du Maine seem dowdy. Not only were there sumptuous entertainments in the house, but the gardens came alive with laughter and smart talk. Always extensive, the gardens now had their French symmetry and order modified in the informal English manner, which meant adding such "follies" as Chinese pagodas. The flower beds included the innovation of a tulip garden and could be enjoyed by all, since this park, like many of the great private ones of the time, even the royal gardens at Versailles, was open to the public. The kitchen garden produced the first nectarines grown in the region and was considered one of "the wonders of Paris."

The Biron estate went to a nephew, the Duc de Lauzun, known for his good looks and gallantry as *beau* Lauzun. Madame Campan, lady of the bedchamber to the Queen, provided an explanation for Lauzun's implacable hatred of Marie-Antoinette. Once during an audience in the Cabinet Doré at Versailles, Lauzun presumed upon his own personal attractions and made advances to the young and beautiful Queen. "Please leave the room sir!" she said, later adding: "I never wish to see that man again." The consort of Louis XVI then took care that Lauzun did not inherit his uncle's command of the French Guards. Come the Revolution, Lauzun joined the party of Philippe-Égalité.

At the height of the Terror, the next owner, the Duc de Chârost, Lauzun's nephew, saved the hôtel from molestation by force of his well-known public-spirited philanthropy. Finally, in 1820, the property was acquired by the nuns of the Sacred Heart, who set up a boarding school for young women of the aristocracy. Among the pupils was Eugénie de Montijo, who would marry Louis-Napoleon and become Empress of France. Sad to say, the nuns sold off the beautiful *boiseries* on the ground floor, viewing them as dispensable vanities. Then with the separation of Church and state in France (1905), the Couvent du Sacré-Coeur, like many other religious institutions, was dissolved.

In 1907, while waiting for the mansion's demolition, a trustee divided up the Hôtel de Biron into several small lodgings, which, because they were set in a garden environment, attracted artists, among them the poet Jean Cocteau, the painter Henri Matisse, the dancer Isadora Duncan, and, most important of all, that master of written German, Rainer Maria Rilke. This tenant, who had earlier served as secretary to the great Auguste Rodin, now encouraged the sculptor to rent several rooms as storage space for his work and collection. Soon, in the autumn glory of his fame, Rodin would be commuting daily from suburban Meudon to work in a spacious studio at the Hôtel de Biron.

Meanwhile, in late spring 1908, the "Académie Matisse" installed itself in the Hôtel de Biron, occupying a large space under the apartment of the Matisses themselves. This art school had been established only the previous autumn by Hans Purrmann, a German follower of Matisse, and Sarah Stein, the sister-in-law of Gertrude and Leo. Their purpose was to help finance Matisse in his own work and to enable students to benefit from instruction under one of the great innovators of 20th-century modernism. Among the Americans who studied there, before the academy closed in 1911, following Matisse's move to a Paris suburb, were Max Weber, Patrick Henry Bruce, Maurice Sterne, and Walter Pach. Two of the other students were French, but most of the class consisted of aspiring young artists from outside France, such as Matthew Smith, now recognized as the best British watercolorist of his generation.

Acquired by the French government in 1910, the Hôtel de Biron became the Musée Rodin in 1916.

Rainer Maria Rilke (1875–1926)

opposite: In the 19th century, while occupied by the boarding school of the Sisters of the Sacred Heart, the Hôtel de Biron lost almost all of its superb 18th-century *boiseries*. Recently, however, the French Historic Monuments Service managed to trace and acquire the paneling originally designed for the two oval salons. Stripped of all finish but nonetheless reinstalled, the paneling, which is in the finest Rococo of the Louis XV period, may yet be repainted and regilded.   **page 182:** The greater sobriety of the carving in the square salon seems more in the manner of the Régence than in that of the Rococo.

Hôtel de Noirmoutier

"Handsome, with a well-turned figure, Monsieur de Noirmoutier was respected for his wit and his ambition, and he made a fine impression when he first went into society," Saint-Simon remembered. "But he was to miss all this before too long." What happened was that the unfortunate Marquis caught smallpox before he was twenty and as a result lost his eyesight. "We can imagine his despair. Once he recovered and returned to Paris, he spent twenty long years without being able to summon up the courage to go out of his house or receive visitors. There he spent his life, depending on friends to read aloud. He had a retentive memory, never forgetting what was once said or read to him, and in this long seclusion, his mind, by nature vigorous and cheerful, was shaped and schooled by reading and reflection. And so he became a philosopher and a man of excellent company when finally he did decide to receive guests."

Fortunately, his fine personal qualities assured him the enduring devotion of a good friend, the Comte de Fiesque, who moved in with Noirmoutier and remained as close to him as the distractions of youth, an army career, and attendance at court would permit. It was Fiesque, mainly, who persuaded the blind man to open his doors to callers. "Gradually," wrote Saint-Simon, "he got used to it, showing himself affable and courteous to all, and the circle grew wider, encompassing acquaintances as well as intimate friends. Some of these confided in him

above: Dating from 1722, when it was built from plans by Jean Courtonne, the Hôtel de Noirmoutier displays on its courtyard façade all the elegance, refinement, and harmonious equilibrium characteristic of the Régence period. Classicism, however, reigns, especially in the lightly projecting central pavilion, with its pilasters, sculptured keystones, and triangular pediment. But the exquisite wrought-iron grilles are distinctively French. **opposite and pages 186–187:** Only the former *chambre de parade* ("state bedroom"), now used as a dining room, has retained its original paneling, albeit cleansed of paint and gilding. The egrets carved into the pilaster capitals derived from the arms of the Trémoilles, to which family the Duc de Noirmoutier belonged.

and shared their affairs at court, in society, and even in the domestic sphere. All found profit in his advice. In short, it became the fashion to be on good terms with Monsieur de Noirmoutier, and everyone who saw him was charmed by his intelligence, his conversation, and his good judgment. . . . His house became a tribunal, and it mattered not whether one was the plaintiff or the defendant. Either as adviser or confidant, the Marquis had a hand in almost everything, and without ever leaving his room, he found himself the best-informed man in Paris in regard to the court as well as to society, much trusted and much relied upon by all his friends."

First married in 1688, Noirmoutier was left a childless widower after eighteen months. He remarried in 1700, taking as his wife the daughter of Duret de Chevry, president of the audit office. Madame Noirmoutier was, we are told, a woman of merit, judgment, and good sense, in whom her husband had confidence and who made up in every way for his blindness. A member of the old and illustrious family of La Trémoille, Noirmoutier was made a Duke and a peer of the realm in 1707. This occurred at the behest of his sister, the Princesse des Ursins, who was then all-powerful with Louis XIV and Madame de Maintenon. This lady also had an enormous influence on Louis XIV's grandson, King Philip V of Spain, and his Queen, whom she served as *camarera mayor*.

After having been Saint-Simon's neighbor in the Rue Saint-Dominque, the Duc de Noirmoutier decided in 1722, at age seventy, to build the house that now bears his name. As architect, he chose Jean Courtonne, who at about the same time was working on the Hôtel Matignon. "The wonder is," wrote Saint-Simon, "that, though not well off, he built a charming house toward the end of the Rue de Grenelle, himself deciding on the layout and proportions from top to bottom, and on everything else, from the doors to the merest utilities, even on the ornamentation, the mirrors, the cornices, and the fireplaces. He also chose the upholstery for the furniture, actually stipulating the colors." It is not known who helped the sightless man in these tricky decisions.

In 1735 the heirs of the Duc de Noirmoutier sold his hôtel to Élisabeth-Alexandrine de Bourbon-Condé. Also known as Mademoiselle de Sens, this proprietress was the daughter of the Duc de Bourbon and the Mademoiselle de Nantes who as "Madame la Duchesse" built the Palais Bourbon. A child worthy of her mother, Mademoiselle de Sens carried on a twenty-year public liaison with the Comte de Langeron. At her death in 1755, the mansion was acquired by the Marquis de Beringhem, whose widow kept it right up to the Revolution. By 1797 a bookstore was being run on the premises by Jean-Baptiste Louvet de Couvray, then well known as the author of a series of singular novels dedicated to the career of a certain Faublas, a character picaresque and amusing enough to disguise himself as a girl in order to have discreet access to the women he desired. Louvet could also be deadly serious, as in 1791 when he went before the legislative assembly to howl that "millions of our fellow citizens have hurled themselves against the feudal regime and can't rest until all such slavery is abolished." Even so, he failed to please Robespierre and found it convenient to go into hiding in 1793. Louvet may have had his finest moment only in the 20th century. The German Count Harry Kessler, one of the age's great cultural arbiters, advised his good friend Hugo von Hofmannsthal to read *Faublas* before undertaking the libretto of Richard Strauss' *Der Rosenkavalier*.

From 1877 on the Hôtel de Noirmoutier housed several major figures in the French military, and in 1919 it was put at the disposal of Marshal Foch, hero of World War I, who died there in 1929. Today it is the official residence of the Prefect of Paris and the Île-de-France.

When built in 1705 from plans by Alexandre Delamair, the Hôtel de Besenval consisted of a single story, entered through a portico of engaged Corinthian columns and embellished with sculptural busts that are still in place. The architect Brongniart added the upper story in 1782, taking care to make a harmonious integration with the earlier structure. Thus, the pilasters above correspond to the more prominent vertical elements below, which support a shallow balcony protected by a handsome wrought-iron grille.

Pierre Victor, Baron de Besenval (1721–94)

Hôtel de Besenval

Connoisseurs of the Rococo already know the charms of the Hôtel de Besenval, where the boudoir, conceived around 1743 by a certain Babel, is a creation of supreme delicacy. The house itself comes from plans designed about 1705 by Alexandre Delamair, who achieved great fame for his work at the Hôtel de Rohan and its neighbor in the Marais, the Hôtel de Soubise. In the Rue de Grenelle the architect's patron was the Abbé Chanac de Pompadour. When first built, the house consisted of nothing but the ground floor. And there the Abbé "kept a footman, almost as old as he, to whom he gave so much a day, in addition to his wages, to read the breviary in the Abbé's stead, and the man floundered through it in a corner of the waiting room. With this, the Abbé apparently considered he had done his duty, just like the canons who pay cantors to substitute for them and sing in the choir." We may presume that it was the Abbé de Pompadour's nieces, the inheritors of the house in 1710, who brought in Babel to contrive the resplendent boudoir.

In 1747 the house fell into the hands of Madeleine-Angélique de Villeroy, widow of the Duc de Boufflers, who in 1750 chose as her second husband the Duc-Maréchal de Luxembourg. They were to earn their place in history, the Luxembourgs, as the patrons of Jean-Jacques Rousseau. "I stood in the greatest awe of Madame de Luxembourg," the great Romantic wrote in his *Confessions*. "I knew that she could be kind. I had seen her several times at the theatre and at the home of Madame Dupin [Rousseau's employer for some time and the mistress of the Hôtel de Lambert, as well as of the Château de Chenonceaux, and an ancestress of the 19th-century novelist George Sand] ten or twelve years before, when she was the Duchesse de Boufflers and still shone in all her early beauty. But she was said to have a wicked tongue, and in so great a lady this reputation made me tremble. Yet, as soon as I saw her I was enthralled. I found her charming with a charm that time cannot alter, the charm most likely to appeal to my heart. I had expected to find her conversation caustic and consisting of one epigram after another. It was not like that; it was something much finer. The talk of Madame de Luxembourg did not sparkle with wit; there were no outbursts of high spirits; nor even what one could properly call finesse. But in her talk there reigned an exquisite delicacy that never obtruded but was always pleas-

above: The small boudoir at the Hôtel de Besenval, with its playful Rococo gilded reliefs on wall panels, on the ceiling, and in the alcove, is one of the most charming creations of 18th-century French architecture. **opposite:** The drawing room, much plainer in its paneling, is partially reflected in a mirror-lined door.

ing. Her compliments were all the more intoxicating for being so simple and direct. It was as if they had slipped out without her having to think about them at all. It was if her heart were overflowing, merely because it had been too full."

Madame de Luxembourg was to sell her town house to Guy Guérapin de Vauréal, Bishop of Rennes, who counted among the many to place low in the esteem of Saint-Simon. "He is a queer fellow," reported the Duke, "but with wit, intrigue of every sort, and unparalleled effrontery, all of which he could use in the most shameless way. He was also rich, but came from the lowest order, and somehow made a place for himself at court. *Son nom est Guérapin et son état franc galopin* ['rank upstart']."

On the Bishop's death in 1760, the heirs leased the house to the Baron de Besenval, inspector general of the Swiss guard employed by the royal family, and then sold it to him in 1767. He added a story and, in an innovation then considered eccentric, had a swimming pool installed in the basement. This was designed by Alexandre-Théodore Brongniart, who found his inspiration in the grottoes of antiquity. The sculptured decorations (now scattered) were carved by none other than Clodion. At the inauguration of this fancy pool—an event carried out with great pomp—Besenval summoned one of the guards to be the first to swim in it. The poor fellow caught a chill and died a few days later.

Besenval was a figure of great fascination for Madame Campan, Marie-Antoinette's lady of the bedchamber. He had, she wrote, "retained all the simplicity of the Swiss and had acquired all the finesse of a French courtier. At fifty, with white hair that led women to trust him, he could never give up indulging in amorous dalliance. He would speak of his native mountains with enthusiasm and, all teary-eyed, profess to like nothing better than singing the songs of Swiss cowherds. Meanwhile, he was also the most agreeable raconteur in the circle of the Comtesse Jules de Polignac [Marie-Antoinette's close friend]. And it was the latest ditty, the latest *bon mot,* and the latest gossip that had to dominate conversation in the Queen's company."

Occasionally, the good Swiss could go too far. "While speaking to me of the strange presumption that men have, and the caution that women must always maintain toward them," Madame Campan recalled, "the Queen added that growing older never deprives them of the hope of pleasing, so long as they can be clever. She had treated the Baron de Besenval like a nice old Swiss gentleman, courteous and witty. Because of his white hair she had thought him a man of no consequence—only to find out she was mistaken. After enjoining me to secrecy, Her Majesty told me that, finding herself one time alone with the Baron, he had begun to pay compliments and make pretty speeches in the most outlandish manner. Quite carried away, he even threw himself on his knees and attempted to make love to her. Cutting these advances short, the Queen said to the Baron: 'Stand up, sir! The King shall know nothing about this behavior that would have disgraced you forever.' The elderly gallant turned white and blurted out an apology, after which Her Majesty left the room without a word and has rarely spoken to him since. . . . As a practiced courtier, he managed to swallow his shame and the resentment he would naturally have felt. And he did not lose his place on the list of those received at Trianon [the park within the park favored by Marie-Antoinette at Versailles]."

Besenval died in 1794, leaving his town house to the Maréchal de Ségur. The latter's son sold the house in 1797 to the Marquise de Chabrillan. Eventually it passed to the Montholon-Semonvilles, from whom the Swiss Confederation acquired the mansion in 1938.

opposite: In the Salon Doré at the Hôtel de Besenval a symmetrical arrangement typical of the 18th century has been observed throughout, in the doors alternating with false doors and in mirrors corresponding to other mirrors and to windows on opposite walls. Here, the Rococo phase of the Louis XV style is at its height. The furniture, which, like the Aubusson carpet, belonged to Baron de Besenval, dates from the reign of Louis XVI.

above: In 1782 Baron de Besenval, commander of the Swiss guard in the employ of the French royal family, had the dining room redecorated in the cool, even severe manner of the emerging Neoclassical style.

Hôtel de Jarnac

Designed in 1784 by Jacques-Guillaume Legrand for a certain Léonard Chapelle, the Hôtel de Jarnac conceals behind its rather grim façade more than one echo of the arabesques fancied in England by the brothers Adam. This should not surprise, since Anglomania, swelling toward the full flood of the Romantic movement, was on the rise throughout the reign of Louis XVI. Marie-Charles-Rosalie de Rohan-Chabot, Comte de Jarnac, did not commission the house to which he lent his name, nor did he ever own it, but rather lived there simply as a lease-holder.

After passing under the control of a variety of tenants, the Hôtel de Jarnac had its best-known occupant in the Comte de Villèle, who arrived in 1828 after having been forced from office as Prime Minister on the eve of the elections of 1827. An ultrarightest intent upon cancelling the effects of the Revolution, he had served under both Restoration monarchs, Louis XVIII and Charles X. If Villèle won fame, no one need envy it. "He has just as many loyal followers as an epidemic would have, if an epidemic could hand out pensions," remarked one of Napoleon's old generals. Thus, even his greatest success—the extraction from the French government of compensation to the titled émigrés for their losses during the Revolution—functioned mainly to condemn Villèle politically. To the beneficiaries of the act, the awards were too long in coming, while to the bourgeoisie, the arrangement meant a financial loss, for the compensation was to be financed by means of reduced interest paid on government bonds. Meanwhile, Villèle's true loyalty was to Charles X, a monarch who could say to the glum crowds that greeted him: "I have not come here to take instruction, but rather to receive your homage." Needless to say, Charles was the last of the Bourbons and, like Villèle, a professional failure.

In 1834 the mansion was acquired by Guillaume Dupuytren, the famed chief of surgery at the Hôtel-Dieu, Paris' municipal hospital. One year later he died, whereupon his daughter sold the property to Pierre Soltykoff, who in turn ceded it to the Duchesse de Valençay in 1847.

In 1821 this lady, born Alix de Montmorency, the sister of the last Duke of an ancient line, had been married at eighteen to eighteen-year-old Louis de Talleyrand-Périgord, the great-nephew of the celebrated

In its extreme simplicity and in the elegance of its proportions, the Hôtel de Jarnac, which dates from 1784, represents the Neoclassical style at its most rigorous and severe. Facing the courtyard **(above)** is a colossal Ionic colonnade supporting an entablature and, above the cornice, an attic. A slightly more lyric note is struck on the garden facade **(opposite),** where the giant engaged columns of the portico are surmounted by an arched pediment. Unfortunately, the architrave was broken in the 19th century for the insertion of larger windows on the upper story.

195

diplomat. The latter had chosen this means to ally himself to the family considered the first in the kingdom. Moreover, Mademoiselle de Montmorency was an heiress of great fortune. Altogether so opportune was the marriage that Charles X saluted it by creating young Louis Duc de Valençay. However, the union proved to have been made in a treaty room more than in heaven, and like most *ententes cordiales,* convenience proved a poor substitute for a really good match. The Valençays turned out to be openly and notoriously unsuited to one another. He was as meek as she was temperamental. Consequently, once her parents were dead in 1846, the Duchess, now long separated from her husband, applied for and received separate maintenance, which meant the control of her own property. Six months later she purchased the Hôtel de Jarnac.

After 1858, when the Duchesse de Valençay died, a succession of owners lived in the mansion. The present proprietor-occupant has recently restored the house.

below: In the dining room flat walls and right angles dominate, except in the overdoors, which are filled with allegorical reliefs. Mirror revetments correspond to the windows in the opposite wall. The painting is a masterpiece of the waterlily series by Monet. Harmonizing with its deep blue-green tonality are the tables covered in goatskin tinted to resemble malachite.

opposite: The main salon in the Hôtel de Jarnac is structured into bays by engaged Ionic columns supporting a corbeled cornice. Where the walls are solid, round-headed false doors lined with mirror reflect the garden outside. Filling the lunettes over the real doors are allegorical reliefs depicting the Four Elements. The wall reliefs between the columns on the left duplicate the arabesque designs in the *chambre de parade* at the Hôtel de Galliffet, a house also designed by Legrand.

197

When built in 1722–28 the Hôtel de Lassay was a long, low Régence structure of a single story. The addition of an upper floor in the 19th century transformed the *hôtel particulier* into a great and stately palace.

Louis-Joseph de Bourbon, Prince de Condé
(1736–1818)

Hôtel de Lassay

A magnificent relic from the Régence period is the Hôtel de Lassay, built between 1722 and 1728 for Léon de Madaillan, Marquis de Lassay. One of the fortunate few who made millions out of speculating in the schemes of the Scotsman John Law, de Lassay is said to have asked Lassurance (Pierre Cailleteau), the trusted assistant of Jules Hardouin-Mansart, to begin the mansion. Other architects, however, were certainly brought in, among them Carlo Giardini, Jacques Gabriel, and Jean Aubert, to whom is generally attributed the grandiose but sober façade. On the interior, a multitude of C-scrolls forming bands of mosaics and cornices loaded with gilded medallions foretell the splendors of the Rococo. And no one, in all likelihood, enjoyed this luxury more than de Lassay's neighbor and mistress, the widowed Duchesse de Bourbon, daughter of Louis XIV and Madame de Montespan. In the last days of *le roi soleil,* de Lassay was nominated minister to Berlin but preferred to stay in Paris at the side of his love. "With the face of a monkey," wrote Saint-Simon, "he was nonetheless a fine figure of a man." The liaison between de Lassay and the Duchess was unusually close; it was also a curiously public affair.

After the death of de Lassay, the mansion passed to his widow and then to his nephew, Louis de Brancas, Comte de Lauraguais, who in 1768 sold it to the Prince de Condé. The latter also owned the Palais Bourbon next door, having just shortly before purchased it from Louis XV. But he preferred the Hôtel de Lassay and thus had it sumptuously fitted out for himself and his son and daughter-in-law.

199

Confiscated during the Revolution, the Hôtel de Lassay housed the École Polytechnique until 1804. With the restoration of the Bourbon monarchy in 1814, the property was returned to the Condés, who held it until the last Prince died in 1830. His heir, the Duc d'Aumale, first rented and then in 1843 sold the house to the French state as the residence of the president of the Chamber of Deputies. Now the mansion would become a true palace, enlarged by an upper story and joined to the Palais Bourbon by means of a vast and stately gallery.

The individual to fill this post and occupy the Hôtel de Lassay with unrivaled flair was the Duc de Morny, the king-maker behind Napoleon III and a personality who, after the Emperor himself, would seem most perfectly to embody the sublime and the ridiculous of the Second Empire. Alphonse Daudet, in his novel *Le Nabab* (1877), wrote: "What one sees from a distance in a building is not its foundation, be it solid or shaky, or its architectural mass. What one sees is its slender gilt spire, sharply outlined, added for the pleasure of the eye. What one saw in France under the Second Empire, and indeed all Europe at the time, was Morny."

Like Louis-Napoleon, Morny was the son of Hortense, Queen of Holland, and therefore the grandson of Joséphine Bonaparte and her first husband, Alexandre de Beauharnais. For a father, however, he had to look to Hortense's lover, the Comte de Flahaut, which more than likely made him the grandson of Talleyrand, whose shrewd business sense he certainly possessed. After an army career, in which he fought in North Africa, Morny entered politics and was elected a deputy in 1842, at the same time that he gained a strategic position in the financial and industrial world under the bourgeois King, Louis-Philippe.

But if Morny created Napoleon III, there was one who claimed to have been the creator of Morny himself. This was the beautiful and wealthy Comtesse Le Hon, daughter of the Brussels banker Mosselman and wife of the Belgian ambassador to France. Everyone knew about the liaison of Morny and the *ambassadrice;* thus, no shock of surprise was felt when, next door to the Countess' own hôtel at the Champs-Elysées, he built a small house for himself, which quickly became known as *la niche à Fidele* ("Fido's kennel"). Here the pair led an idyllic existence, until Morny decided he must marry, alleging: "The Emperor wishes it, and France desires it." Without sympathy for either the Emperor or France, Madame Le Hon considered the desertion more than a lover's betrayal, really an unforgivable act of indelicacy. Since their finances, as well as their affections, were closely knit, the Emperor had to intervene and make certain that the parties received satisfaction without the scandal of a court proceeding. Still, believing herself to have been the making of Morny, Madame Le Hon declared: "When I took him up, he was only a Second Lieutenant; I left him a General."

Meanwhile, Morny was exceedingly busy elsewhere. In 1851 he master-minded the *coup d'état* that gave his half-brother dictatorial powers. Then in 1852, as minister of the interior, he used mass intimidation to assure the outcome of the plebiscite that made Bonaparte Napoleon III, Emperor of the French. Morny's reward came when he was created Duke and subsequently became president of the legislative assembly, which placed him in the Hôtel de Lassay. Now the mansion entered its most brilliant period, with *fête* following *fête* in gaudy, extravagant succession. In 1855 a grand reception, graced by the Emperor and Empress, cost a fortune, none of which was paid by the crafty host, who had taken the precaution of having the Chamber of Deputies declare the soirée an official one. The most memorable event, however, occurred the following year, when Morny gave a ball in honor of Queen Maria

Louise-Françoise, Duchesse de Bourbon (d. 1743)

opposite: The great gallery, or Salle des Fêtes, at the Hôtel de Lassay connects this mansion, which is the residence of the president of the French legislative assembly, to the Palais Bourbon, where the deputies sit. Built in the 19th century, the hall is typical of Second Empire taste in its eclectic borrowings from every manner of historical style. To the discomfort of purists, the hall tends to seduce by its overpowering scale and ostentatious splendor.

Christina of Spain. With the Rococo period as the prescribed theme, the guests came wearing powdered hair, and as they waltzed about the grand gallery—in a vigorous, whirling 19th-century dance totally unlike the sedate minuets of the *ancien régime*—the powder flew into the air, transforming it into haze. Said Morny: "If we were not dancing on a volcano, certainly we seemed to be in the dust of one."

The very model of the Second Empire parvenu grandee, Morny did fabulously well in the stock market and even wrote boulevard comedies, most of them critical flops but one, at least, set to music by *the* composer of the age, Jacques Offenbach. To add further to the era's mood of opulent pleasure, Morny took it upon himself to transform Deauville from a sad and ignored resort into a watering place even more fashionable than neighboring Trouville.

The woman Morny decided to marry was Princess Sophie Troubetzkoi, whom he met while in Saint Petersberg in 1856 as special envoy to the coronation of Alexander II. Although a ravishing beauty, the young Duchesse de Morny proved ill suited to the official life that awaited her in France. Protesting that "the Slavic soul needs space to move about in," she resented the political crowds her husband was compelled to invite. She found them *prostoi* or "vulgar," and she showed it. Preferring the company of animals, she filled the Hôtel de Lassay with a menagerie of exotic beasts, from monkeys and rare birds to tiny Japanese dogs. For human society, she cultivated a few intimates and had them to her boudoir for a quiet smoke.

One of these—a poor young woman of good family brought to Paris from Russia by the Duchesse de Morny—became the subject of a farce worthy of a theatre on the new boulevards built by Baron Haussmann. In love with his wife, but equally fond of escapades, the Duke decided to have one on an afternoon when he and the Russian companion found themselves alone in the Hôtel de Lassay. But the Duchess returned suddenly and, of course, caught the pair *flagrante delicto,* which precipitated a scene of truly tragicomic dimensions. But the Mornys made up, and when the Duke died in 1865, worn out by a ceaseless round of politics, business, and pleasure, the Duchess cut off her long blond tresses and placed them in her husband's coffin. Later a friendly enemy would observe: "[Morny's] last clever trick was to die in time"—two years before the disaster of the French invasion of Mexico and five years before the still greater disaster of the Franco-Prussian War, which brought an abrupt end to the *opéra bouffe* Second Empire. France renewed and relished its *belle époque* for almost another half-century, but not until 1918 did it recover the provinces of Alsace and Lorraine, the war prizes taken by a victorious Germany in 1870–71.

The former music room in the Hôtel de Lassay seems to have retained nothing of its original 18th-century décor. Even the gilded relief work on the cornice is a Second Empire pastiche imitating the Rococo style. The Gobelins tapestry occupying the entire wall opposite the windows is a re-creation of Raphael's *School of Athens,* a monumental fresco in Rome's Vatican Palace. On either side of the door leading to the Salle des Fêtes are two superb *torchères* cast in bronze and partially gilded.

opposite: The 19th-century changes made in the décor of the Hôtel de Lassay's reception room were so sweeping that it is difficult to detect what may remain of the original 18th-century elements beneath the "enrichments" laid on by the Second Empire. Obviously of the latter era are the fireplaces, the overdoor paintings, and the plate glass mirrors.   **below:** According to old inventories, this salon was hung in the 18th century with Lyons silks. The paneling now on the walls was copied in the 19th century from the grand salon reproduced opposite.

The Champs-Élysées
and the Faubourg Saint-Honoré

Hôtel de Chârost
Hôtel de Toulouse
Palais de l'Élysée
Hôtel de Païva

At the Hôtel de Chârost, a gilt-bronze centerpiece
created by Thomire

Hôtel de Chârost

The Hôtel de Chârost has been occupied by the British Embassy since August 22, 1814, when the Duke of Wellington arrived to deal with the abdication of Napoleon. In that time the noble spaces of this Régence mansion have harbored a goodly number of eccentrics from across the Channel. And thus it should be, according to Cynthia Gladwyn, whose husband was Ambassador from 1954 to 1960. "The French," she wrote in *The Paris Embassy,* "believe us to be a nation of eccentrics, a character-istic for which they have a lurking admiration."

One envoy completely up to French expectations was Lord Bertie of Thane, who served in Paris from 1905 to 1918. Outrageously rude to nearly everyone, but never to Georges Clémenceau, the wartime Prime Minister with whom he hit it off at all times, Lord Bertie was remembered for his vast collection of pornographic drawings. Following him in 1918–20 was the Earl of Derby, "said to look like a shorthorn bull." "My dear Curzon," Lord Derby wrote one afternoon to the Foreign Secretary, "I have always known you to be a cad. I now know that you are a liar." The diplomatic staff, true to form, retrieved the letter from the courier pouch, and by the next morning the Ambassador had recovered himself. Then there was Lord Tyrell, whose tenure lasted from 1928 to 1934. He gained a reputation as the opponent of the written word. "If you put things on paper, people will get at your," he warned.

An enormously congenial Ambassador was Alfred Duff Cooper, whom Churchill appointed to the post in Paris immediately after World War II (1944–47). A great asset to Cooper's career was his wife, Lady Diana Manners, the daughter of the Duke of Rutland and a fabled beauty who starred in Max Reinhardt's production of *The Miracle.* Duff

Cooper even got along with de Gaulle, despite the anxiety this caused in Sir Winston. As the civilized biographer of Talleyrand, Cooper had all the glamour of a working intellectual and writer, which in the Hôtel de Chârost, a bastion of aristocratic nonchalance, may have made him seem the greatest eccentric of all. He even introduced a well-stocked library. To carry out this project, Cooper summoned the architect Georges Geffroy and listened to the advice of Le Corbusier's friend, the South American millionaire Charles de Beistegui. In the very special room that came forth the shelves are fringed in green silk, supplementing the green carpet and black-banded green velvet curtains, all selected by the painter Christian Bérard. Here one could forget the dark day in 1940 when the embassy was closed, and Sir Charles, the mission's Press Counselor, and Lady Mendl (the American decorator and hostess Elsie de Wolfe) set off for Spain in their Rolls, followed by a station wagon heaped high with Vuitton luggage.

Under Duff Cooper (later Viscount Norwich) and Lady Diana the British Embassy in Paris shone with a rare brilliance, and the Hôtel de Chârost was worthy of the compliment. The edifice dates from 1722 and rose from designs by Antoine Mazin, the architect who put the finishing touches on the Hôtel Matignon. In the Rue du Faubourg Saint-Honoré the patron was Armand de Béthune, third Duc de Chârost, Captain of the Royal Guard in 1711, tutor to young Louis XV in 1722, and by 1830 head of the Board of Finance. His mother was the daughter of the great Nicolas Fouquet—the finance minister under young Louis XIV who, before his tragic fall from power, discovered much of the talent that brought greatness to Louis' reign. After the disgrace of her gifted and charismatic father, the Duchesse de Béthune had good reason to be serious and reflective. This made her an intimate of Madame Guyon, the high priestess of mystical quietism, and of this lady's disciple, Fénelon, Archbishop of Cambrai and tutor to the Duc de Bourgogne, Louis XV's father. We may assume, therefore, that the Duc de Chârost had a strict and moral upbringing. Saint-Simon all but confirms it, calling Chârost a man of "scrupulous integrity and much honor." But he was also, in the opinion of the chronicler, intensely ambitious, even given to fits of jealousy, and only too found of society, where he was widely received and where he always behaved with great decorum. "He may be," Saint-Simon goes on, "the only man who knew how to combine a publicly professed, lifelong faith and the very closest relations with freethinkers, as well as with almost everyone else. His company was sought on all sides, and out of respect for him—certainly not in mockery—no debauchery occurred at the parties he attended, even in court and army circles where the mores were quite different from his. Yet no one felt constrained in either gaiety or personal liberty. Indeed he was good and convivial company, witty, cheerful, and capable of the most apt and pleasant comments. His piety seemed to function as a stern break upon a naturally vivacious temperament, resulting in great force of character, which some liked to tease."

Chârost's grandson, the fourth Duke, succeeded to the estate in 1745 and lived at the hôtel until 1785, when he leased it to the Comte de La Marche, the wealthy landowner who laid out the English garden and redecorated the central salon on the ground floor. His designer may have been the great Victor Louis, whose opera house in Bordeaux is one of the triumphs of the Louis XVI style. La Marche was also the close friend of Honoré-Gabriel, Comte de Mirabeau, whose enormous vocabulary made him the great orator of the early days of the Revolution, before it was discovered that he had all along been in the pay of the court. Until his death on April 2, 1791, Mirabeau was to serve as the middle man between the royal family and the Revolutionary leaders. As for the Duc de Chârost, he landed in prison during the Terror, but his long-practiced and well-known philanthropy saved him from the guillotine. He died in 1800, the victim of smallpox while he was caring for the sick of Paris' *premier arrondissement* (bordering on the Tuileries Gardens), of which he has been elected mayor.

Three years later, in 1803, Madame de Chârost sold the mansion to Pauline Bonaparte, Napoleon's beautiful and independent sister and the widow of General Leclerc. Mourning was not the style of Pauline, and as soon as the law allowed, she threw off her weeds and donned a wedding gown, this time to marry Prince Camillo Borghese, scion of old Roman nobility. But she was ill rewarded for an impatience that thoroughly aroused the Emperor's wrath. The Prince proved to be tedious. "I would rather have remained a widow with 20,000 francs a year," complained Pauline, "than become the wife of a eunuch." Seeing as little as possible of this husband, she consoled herself with many lovers, all of which distressed Napoleon, who was as moralistic about her escapades as he was indulgent of his own.

It was at the Hôtel de Chârost that Napoleon had his rendez-vous with Madame de Mathis, the wife of a Piedmontese nobleman and lady-in-waiting to Pauline. The latter, who detested Joséphine, had introduced Madame de Mathis with malice of forethought. To the surprise of both sister and brother, the opulent blond beauty showed an unexpected resistance to the Emperor's advances. Lectured by Pauline on her duty, Madame de Mathis did consent to a secret meeting but refused to grant what her suitor desired. Upon which Napoleon and Pauline discussed

This superb library at the Hôtel de Chârost was installed after World War II by Ambassador Duff Cooper, whose collaborators on the project were architect Georges Geffroy, the designer Charles de Beistegui, and the painter Christian Bérard. All worked in the Neoclassical mode that Pauline Bonaparte-Borghese had so triumphantly brought to the mansion, now the British Embassy, almost a century and a half earlier.

the problem in a series of thirty-four letters, the very last of which records the surrender of Madame de Mathis.

Pauline always had a mind of her own. She liked being carried into her bath by a tall Negro whom she had christened herself and then married off to one of her chambermaids. If her feet were cold, she would warm them against the breast of one of her ladies-in-waiting, who to render the service, lay prone upon the floor. Pauline's beauty, acknowledged by all contemporaries, was immortalized by the Italian sculptor Canova, who represented her as *Venus Victrix*, naked to the hips. When asked whether she minded posing in the nude for Canova, she replied with the utmost candor: "Not at all. The studio was well heated." The life-size statue of a half-recumbent Pauline has long been a luminous presence among the Renaissance and Baroque treasures of Rome's Palazzo Borghese.

Pauline made a number of improvements to the Hôtel de Chârost, adding a wing on the garden side of the ground floor in which she hung some of the finest paintings in the Borghese collection. And room after room was redecorated by Pierre Fontaine, codesigner with Charles Percier of the Rue de Rivoli, Malmaison, the Napoleonic Louvre, and so many other buildings and interiors of the Empire period. Three waiting rooms appeared on the ground floor, in addition to a dining room lit by splendid chandeliers, a yellow drawing room, a hall of honor in poppy-red velvet, and a state bedroom in blue satin, complemented by a boudoir. In these glorious chambers, on every Wednesday evening, Pauline would stage parties of desperate splendor.

Yet Pauline Bonaparte-Borghese did not have too good a time. To the Duchesse d'Abrantès, Napoleon's sister failed as a hostess. "She was too indolent and took no care of anything, save her own dress and person." The victim of Napoleon's "imperial system," she had her guest lists drawn up by General Duroc, master of the imperial household. "It was worth hearing Duroc," the Duchesse d'Abrantès tells us, "when he de-

above: The life-size, semirecumbent portrait statue of Pauline Bonaparte, the sister of Napoleon and the wife of Prince Camillo Borghese, was carved in gleaming white marble by Antonio Canova in 1808. He represented his subject as *Venus Victrix.* The work has long stood among the Renaissance and Baroque treasures of the Palazzo Borghese in Rome.   **opposite:** The gilt-wood bed commissioned by Pauline still stands in her bedroom at the Hôtel de Charost. Here reflected in her bronze-fitted mirror, it is seen to be decorated with standing Egyptian figures and crowned *à la polonaise.* The crimson damask now on the walls replaces the blue satin described in contemporary accounts.

opposite: A handsome drawing room on the ground floor of the Hôtel de Chârost has preserved several elements from the time of Pauline Bonaparte, mainly the fireplace and the gilded chairs and settees, all in the Empire style. In the early 19th century, however, the panels between the Corinthian pilasters, which are now gilded, were probably hung with silk. **below:** The throne room, which occupies the space of Pauline Bonaparte's boudoir, was prepared for Queen Victoria when she visited Paris as a guest of Napoleon III and Empress Eugénie.

scribed the way Pauline would try to wheedle and coax him into striking off the list the name of some woman too pretty for her liking. She was so ingratiating that he could not refuse her. But a sense of fairness would make him hesitate, and then he would say: 'Why remove her name? Are there ever too many good-looking women?' 'Well,' she would answer, 'I'll be there, shan't I, and you'll be able to see me better without her.' "

Such was her loyalty that Pauline, alone of the whole Bonaparte family, accompanied Napoleon into his first exile on the island of Elba. It was then that she sold the Hôtel de Chârost and all its contents to the Duke of Wellington, Britain's Ambassador in France. In these surroundings Wellington could not but give lavish receptions of his own, some of which brought out the raillery in Madame de Boigne. "As generalissimo of the occupying armies . . . [he] did us all the honors at our expense. He gave parties fairly often at which it was indispensable to be present. He wished to have plenty of people and, as our fate largely depended on keeping him in good humor, there was nothing to do but bear with his often freakish whims."

If the French wished to find grounds on which to resent the British, they might well discover them in the modifications made to the interior of the Hôtel de Chârost. Among the offenses, however, must not be counted the winter gallery fashioned on the garden side in 1825 by Visconti, the future architect of the New Louvre. But what can one say for

the throne room, made up from Pauline Bonaparte's boudoir and designed as an extension of the ballroom? It is pure Victorian. Toward the end of the 19th century other parts of the mansion succumbed to what the French term *le plus pur style Louis XVI-Ritz*, but in English it is pure Edwardian. On the whole, however, the British have maintained the Hôtel de Chârost with love and scrupulous care.

Hôtel de Toulouse

If Versailles should be beyond reach, then the visitor to Paris interested in a palace evoking the last days of Louis XIV (who died on September 1, 1715) could well settle for the Hôtel de Toulouse. There, little survives from the 17th and 18th centuries save the grand Galerie Dorée of 1718–19, a gilded, illusionistic, Baroque marvel created by Robert de Cotte, the brother-in-law of Jules Hardouin-Mansart, and the sculptor Antoine Vassé. Although the Galerie Dorée does not possess the vast dimensions of the Hall of Mirrors at Versailles, its lavish splendor is certainly to the royal taste.

The history of the Hôtel de Toulouse, which since 1810 has been the headquarters of the Banque de France, is a long one, complicated in the late 18th century by the unhappy career of Marie-Antoinette's loyal friend, the Princesse de Lamballe. The commission for the mansion came in 1635 from Louis I de Phélypeaux, Marquis de La Vrillière. Secretary of State under Louis XIII, Louis I sprang from an old family of the *noblesse de la robe* that in subsequent generations would produce the naval ministers Pontchartrain and Maurepas, whose names are immor-

A masterwork of the Régence period is the décor of the Galerie Dorée by Robert de Cotte, executed in the Hôtel de Toulouse about 1720. The hall had been built and decorated almost a century earlier, around 1640, when François Perrier painted the illusionistic ceiling in *grisaille*. Under de Cotte this vast composition was colored. Also from the original installation were the large canvases on the walls, by such Italian masters of the Baroque as Pietro da Cortona and Guido Reni, which de Cotte had set in wood paneling carved by François-Antoine Vassé. The tall mirrors opposite the windows, added in the 18th-century, were inspired by Versailles' Hall of Mirrors, which was built well after the Hôtel de Toulouse. In a restoration of about 1870–75 the paintings by the Italians were taken to the Louvre and replaced by copies.

The grand salon in the Hôtel de Toulouse, graced by Fragonard's Rococo masterpiece, *The Fair at Saint-Cloud* (1775).

talized in the geography of Louisiana. To create his town house, Louis I engaged the services of the great François Mansart, who also designed Louis' magnificent Château de Pontchartrain in the Île-de-France. Almost a century later, in 1712, the mansion became the Hôtel de Toulouse when Louis II de La Vrillière, the founder's grandson, got through a moment of financial embarrassment by selling the Parisian property to the Comte de Toulouse, the legitimatized son of Louis XIV and Madame de Montespan. Here was the ideal patron for de Cotte and Vassé, a man who enjoyed every possible advantage. Made an admiral at the age of five, he had become Lieutenant General in the army by the time he was nineteen. When Louis XIV died in 1715 the Comte de Toulouse was master of the royal hunt and chief of the naval council, and had served as governor of both Guyenne and Brittany. Remarkably, the Prince also enjoyed the favor of that elitist, Saint-Simon, who as a member of the Regency council helped save the royal bastard from the official degradation imposed upon his brother, the Duc du Maine. Feeling generous, Saint-Simon wrote: "He was as gracious as his natural coldness would permit. And his integrity went a long way to make up for his want of intelligence. Besides, he proved diligent in dealing with the navy and the merchant marine." In another stroke of luck—extraordinary for the time—the Comte de Toulouse succeeded in marrying the woman he loved. While taking the waters at Bourbon, the Prince met and found himself drawn to the Marquise de Gondrin, a ravishing young widow to whom Saint-Simon could grant a few points, even though she was the sister of the Duc de Noailles, a man the chronicler considered no better than a reptile. But high-born though she was, Madame de Gondrin would not have been acceptable to the Regent—the Duc d'Orléans—as the spouse of a royal Prince, and so the marriage to Toulouse had to be celebrated secretly in the private chapel of the bride's uncle, Cardinal de Noailles, Archbishop of Paris. The day after the Regent died in 1732 the Comte de Toulouse publicly declared his marriage. Following his death in 1737, the Comtesse de Toulouse gained importance at court when, to ingratiate herself with Louis XV, she played the role of protectress to the three Neslé sisters, whose charms held the King in thrall. One of the sisters, the Duchesse de Châteauroux, felt so sure of her power that she forced the smitten monarch to scratch hour after hour at her locked door. In the 19th century the brothers Goncourt speculated that the story of these three women reveals how mistresses ruined the ideal of royalty by turning the King into a vile creature.

The Comte and Comtesse de Toulouse had one son, the Duc de Penthièvre, who inherited all his father's wealth, which by then was immense. A cultivated man with a taste for educated and creative society, the Duc de Penthièvre was also kind and generous toward all who served him in his houses and on his many estates. Thus, when the Revolution broke out, he and his vast properties were left unmolested. Alas, nothing of the sort can be said of his daughter-in-law, the hapless Princesse de Lamballe.

Like his father, the Duc de Penthièvre had only one son, the Prince de Lamballe, who died in 1768 after a brief but utterly debauched life. He left a young widow, Marie-Thérèse de Savoie-Carignan. The Princesse de Lamballe made her appearance at court two years after the death of her wretched husband. And so attractive was the appearance— "like spring wrapped in marten and ermine," wrote Madame de Campan—that some courtiers thought the Princess might marry Louis XV. She was only twenty, and she was fascinating because of her unhappy marriage. She also possessed wisdom, and told Madame du Barry that she had no intention of taking her place in the King's affections. The equally young and fresh Marie-Antoinette seems immediately to have appreciated the virtues of the Princesse de Lamballe, and for her reconstituted the lapsed office of household superintendent.

When the brothers Goncourt came to write the biography of Marie-Antoinette, they too fell under the spell of the Princesse de Lamballe. Her soul, they testified, was as serene as her face. She had delicacy and was an endearing creature, prepared for every sacrifice, faithful even in small things, and never mindful of herself. Although capable of forgetting her own rank, she never forgot that the Queen was Queen. The great age of sensibility had arrived, and the Princesse de Lamballe took it as a personal mission to avoid evil in the world and to dispell all unpleasant thoughts with the sweet charity of her illusions. This enabled her to promote conversation that preserved the Queen in the peace and quiet of a perfect climate. Yet it was also an age of skepticism and satire, and there were those who made fun of the Princess' kindness and saw it as mindless sentimentality. Once, when she and the Queen went boating on the Seine and traveled all the way from Choisy to the Arsenal on the outskirts of Paris, a few passing boatmen recognized the royal party and thought to entertain the ladies by diving into the river. Taken by surprise, the Queen imagined that the men had fallen in and were in danger of drowning. She fainted, and, out of sheer sympathy, the Princesse de Lamballe swooned as well. The incident provoked a cruel comment from Marie-Antoinette's mother, the Empress Maria-Theresa: "The exaggerated fright exhibited by the Princess at the sight of a few boatman in the water strikes me as nothing but humbug."

Yet, when the Revolution came, the Princesse de Lamballe showed not only her latent strength of character but also her complete devotion to Marie-Antoinette. After emigrating to England, she voluntarily returned to France to stand by the Queen in the face of the dangers that thronged about her. On August 10, 1792, after the mob had stormed the Tuileries Palace, the Princesse de Lamballe followed her friend when she and the royal family were imprisoned in the Temple. There the Princess was arrested and removed to another prison, La Force, where in September, following a trial at which she refused to obtain her own release by swearing hatred of the crown, a mob seized her, stripped her naked, severed her head with a butcher knife, and mutilated the body, dragging it in the gutter. With bestiality rampant, it was decided to mount the head on a pike and bear it in triumph to the Temple, there to force the Queen to encounter her trusted friend one last time. A courtier blocked the window and spared Marie-Antoinette the horror outside.

The Revolutionary government confiscated the Hôtel de Toulouse and in it established the national printing works, which gave way to the Banque de France once this institution was founded by Napoleon in 1810. Modifications made to the mansion in the 19th century left little of the façades and décor as they existed in the previous two centuries. The single, outstanding exception is the Galerie Dorée, which survives in a heavily restored state. The hôtel also contains a collection of handsome period furniture and an authentic masterpiece—Fragonard's ever-fresh *Fair at Saint-Cloud*, a celebration of life as it was known by the privileged few, like the Princesse de Lamballe, before the fall of the Bastille.

The polished mahogany paneling in the dining room of the Hôtel de Toulouse makes a handsome setting for the Empire furniture. The tapestries set into the paneling are from the 17th century. On the sideboard stand various pieces of gilt bronze by Pierre-Philippe Thomire.

A 19th-century reconstruction in the Louis XV manner, this splendid room in the Hôtel de Toulouse displays a series of early 18th-century tapestries whose arabesque patterns reflect the designs of Audran and Berain. On the Savonnerie carpet stand a rolltop desk veneered in satinwood and decorated with gilt-bronze fittings, a 17th-century gilt-wood table with marquetry by Boulle, and a set of Louis XV chairs.

Caroline Murat (1782–1839),
Queen of Naples (1808–15)

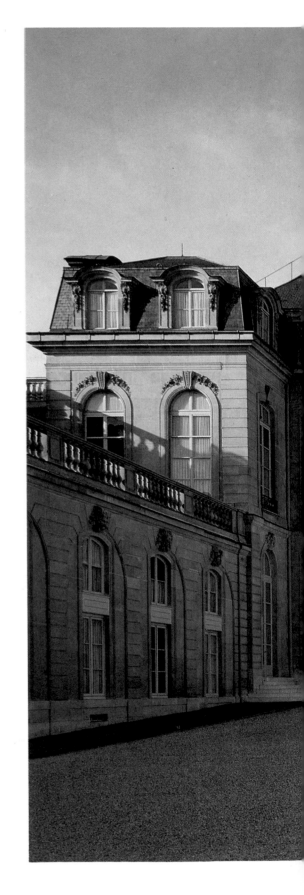

Palais de l'Élysée

Since 1872 the official residence of the President of the Republic, the Palais de l'Élysée seems to have been a way station for everyone traveling the main route into French history, from Madame de Pompadour to the Empress Eugénie. Almost all the occupants left their mark on the mansion; yet it survives both inside and out as a magnificent tribute to French mastery of architectural elegance and decorative refinement.

The Élysée originated as the Hôtel d'Évreux, built in 1722 by Armand-Charles Mallet for Henri de La Tour d'Auvergne, Comte d'Évreux and the grand-nephew of Turenne, often regarded as the greatest of all French generals. When Saint-Simon turned his skeptical attention to the Comte d'Évreux, he wrote: "He had nothing in common with Turenne, except for being of all men of his rank the sliest, while pretending to be the most straightforward. With a mind below the average, he was nevertheless most cunning, ever ready to use underhanded methods to attain his ends." In 1707, to restore his family's fortunes, the Comte d'Évreux married the richest heiress of the day, the daughter of Antoine Crozat, the banker and Maecenas of the arts to whom history owes a debt for his patronage of the great and unhappy painter Antoine Watteau. With all the cleverness cited by Saint-Simon, Évreux ingratiated himself with the Comte de Toulouse, the son of Louis XIV and Madame de Montespan, which then assured a good standing with the old King himself. After Louis' death in 1715, he proved versatile enough to capture the favor of the Regent and, moreover, to make mountains of money out of the speculative schemes of the Scottish economist John Law.

Now relieved of the ugly glassed-in porch erected in the 19th century by Louis-Napoleon during his presidential days, the Élysée Palace retains on its courtyard side all the Régence, classicizing elegance given it in 1718 by the originating architect, Armand-Charles Mollet. Particularly fine is the central pavilion, which projects slightly and provides access, behind the Doric colonnade, to an open but recessed vestibule. At the second level Corinthian pilasters flank classical busts on scroll consoles and at the center a tall arched window decorated with a wrought-iron grille and a sculptured keystone. The whole is crowned by a triangular pediment and a dormered Mansart roof, that hallmark of classic French architecture.

Madame de Pompadour (1721–64)

opposite: Ostentatious in both scale and lavish décor, the Salle des Fêtes is typical of the bourgeois taste of the late 19th-century Third Republic, when President Sadi Carnot had the architect Chancel make this huge addition to the Élysée Palace. Giant Ionic columns support an entablature and a clearstory where large lunettes alternate with fleshy, dancing caryatids. These in turn "sustain" a ceiling squared off and encrusted with richly carved and gilded moldings that enframe illusionistic paintings by E. M. G. Dubuffe. Rows of dazzling chandeliers and heavy velvet, lace-trimmed valances complete the elaborate setting in which occurs so much of republican France's ceremonial life.

Now the Comte d'Évreux was ready to summon Mollet and build his town house, which enabled him to move out of the hôtel provided by his father-in-law in the Place Vendôme. For the new residence Mollet was not the only designer involved. According to Fiske Kimball, the American art historian, the magnificent paneling of the grand salon, the study, and the second waiting room should be attributed to Gilles-Marie Oppenord, the Dutch-born architect who lived most of his life in the shadow of Jules Hardouin-Mansart, only to move suddenly to the first rank once he had been taken into the Crozat circle. Captivated by what he had glimpsed of Borromini's work in Rome, Oppenord was a revolutionary in the art of decoration. Thanks to the exciting quality of his ideas, no one objected too much when the addition he provided to Crozat's town house caved in, or when his work on a tower at Saint-Sulpice had to be removed because it placed too much weight on the structural arches. To the taste of the Régence (1715–23), what mattered were the undulating curves that Oppenord favored, therein foretelling the experiments of Germain Boffrand at the Hôtel de Soubise, where the Rococo truly took form.

In the meantime, troubles began to develop for the seemingly lucky Comte d'Évreux. His wife left him, complaining, so the gossip ran, that her marriage had never been consummated. Crozat demanded back the dowry, which Évreux surrendered, all the while retaining the interest he had received on it. This, he said, was just return for the honor he had done in giving the bourgeois' daughter "such a great name." After a long life dedicated to the pursuit of ambition and pleasure, the Comte d'Évreux died in 1753, pestered by senility and cursed by apoplectic fits.

Now to the Hôtel d'Évreux—or Élysée Palace, as we know it—came its most famous and, in many respects, its most distinguished occupant, the Marquise de Pompadour. "History will forget what manner of woman she was," wrote her biographers, the brothers Goncourts. "We shall think of the mistress of Louis XV as a radiant and charming shadow, seated on one of Boucher's clouds, surrounded by the muses of painting, sculpture, architecture, engraving, music—in fact of all the fine arts." But the effect she had on the house was not great, restricted mainly to alterations on the ground floor, made under the supervision of Lassurance the younger (Jean Cailleteau). Madame de Pompadour was busy elsewhere, mainly at Versailles, where her onerous task was to amuse a chronically bored Louis XV. And a good part of her program was devoted to fixing up an endless string of country houses, beginning with Bellevue and Crécy, both of which have vanished, and including the tiny but surprising Celle-Saint-Cloud near Versailles, the Hermitage the great Gabriel designed for her at Fontainebleau, Menars, to which she paid only one visit, and the Château de Champs, which she rented from the Duc de La Vallière and greatly improved. The Marquise did not need to be told the value of Gabriel, for she offered 100,000 *livres* of her own money to speed the completion of his École Militaire in Paris.

Painted by Boucher, Quentin de La Tour, and Drouais, sculpted by Pigalle, Falconet, and Jean-Baptiste Lemoyne, Madame de Pompadour could be said to have neglected none of the arts. The great factory she launched at Sèvres more than achieved its purpose, which was to create porcelain of a quality to challenge the prestige of the ware made in Dresden. And for her, intellectuals were nothing to shy away from. Jean-Jacques Rousseau became "my owl," and she had his opera *The Village Soothsayer* performed at Fontainebleau and at Bellevue, where she herself took the role of Colin. When it came to Voltaire, he dedicated his play *Tancrède* to her and could not help realizing that he owed her his position as historian to the King. She also saw to it that he wrote *Le Temple*

de la gloire to celebrate France's victory over England at Fontenoy in 1745. The Marquise was even close to the *philosophes,* the freethinkers behind the *Encyclopédie* planned and prepared by Diderot and d'Alembert. "We shall miss her as long as we live," cried Voltaire on her death at forty from consumption (1764). "It is the end of a dream."

Madame de Pompadour willed the mansion to Louis XV, specifying: "I beg him to accept as a present this house, which might make a suitable palace for one of his grandsons. I should wish it to be for His Royal Highness, the Comte de Provence [the future Louis XVIII]." But sensibilities less refined than the Marquise's were now in control, and the hôtel soon became a warehouse, where all the furniture from her various residences was collected and put on sale. From Prussia appeared a major purchaser, Frederick the Great. "I can truthfully say," he declared, "that each of these pieces has cost me a battle in the field, for each embodies the ardor with which that beautiful woman sent French battalions against me, battalions that, luckily for our side, were commanded by officers of her own choosing." The house then continued as a warehouse, filled with royal possessions awaiting the completion of the quarters Gabriel was preparing for them in the Place de la Concorde (now the Naval Ministry).

Sold by Louis XV in 1773 to his controller general of finance, the house was immediately resold to Nicolas Beaujon, a financier who dabbled in art and philanthropy. Beaujon did little to change the décor, but he enlarged the private apartments and redesigned the gardens *à l'anglaise.* Aging and infirm, he spent most of his days lying in bed, watched over by a number of attentive young women he called his "cradle rockers." Beaujon made them all kinds of presents, in return for which he merely insisted that they remain faithful to their husbands. Perhaps he meant this, for in 1784, two years before he died, the old capitalist founded the Beaujon Hospital near the Elysée Palace and a school for the education of twenty-four indigent children.

Beaujon bequeathed the Élysée to Louis XVI, who promptly sold it to Louise-Marie-Thérèse-Bathilde d'Orléans, Duchesse de Bourbon. Her husband was the last of the Condés, but she failed to appreciate him and he her. One day when she was preparing to join Condé at Chantilly, the Duchess received a note saying: "It is unnecessary, Madame, for you to take the trouble of coming out here, because you are as much disliked by my father as by myself and all society."

In the hope of changing her luck in love, the Duchesse de Bourbon now consulted Friedrich Anton Mesmer, the Austrian physician and inventor of animal magnetism, whose treatments required patients to gather in a dimly lit room and there to touch hands while he "mesmerized" them—that is, stroked their bodies with a magnet. In a more worthwhile effort, the Duchess took as a house guest Louis-Claude, Marquis de Saint-Martin, a mystic whose ideas influenced Herber and the German Romantic movement in general.

Arrested during the Terror, the Duchesse de Bourbon owed her life only to the downfall of Robespierre. Having leased her house to a speculator named Hovyn, she sold it to him when the Directory exiled her to Spain. Hovyn turned the ground floor into a dance hall and the grounds into a pleasure garden, where he set up rustic cottages in imitation of the "hamlet" built by the Duchess at Chantilly, who herself had imitated Marie-Antoinette in the pastoral games the Queen liked to play at Trianon. In a further change, Hovyn divided the upper floors of the house into apartments, in one of which would live a boy named Alfred de Vigny, the future poet and lion of the Romantic movement, who in his youth was amazed by the Vanity Fair that passed, shamelessly, along the streets in the neighborhood of the Élysée.

In the summer of 1805 the house acquired a new and spectacular owner, Joachim Murat, one of Napoleon's greatest generals and the husband of Caroline Bonaparte, the Emperor's sister. Already created Grand Duke of Berg, Murat would become King of Naples from 1808 until Napoleon's final surrender in 1815. In 1806 Caroline joined him at the Élysée, now restored and refurnished in the stunning manner of the Empire. Like all of Napoleon's sisters, Caroline was required to give a reception every week, with Friday scheduled as her day. And as the "imperial system" demanded, the guest lists, running to 100 or 200 names, were drawn up by Marshal Duroc, master of the imperial household. The ball that Caroline gave in 1807 in honor of the marriage of her brother Jérôme, King of Westphalia, to Princess Catherine of Württemberg entered the annals as one of the most unforgettable events of the Empire. The banquet itself was historic, prepared by the great Carême and described by him in detail in his book, *Le Cuisinier français* (1833).

When Murat left Paris to assume the throne at Naples, Napoleon took over the Élysée for his own needs. It was, he said, "my sanatorium," less pompous than the Tuileries. On divorcing Joséphine, he gave her the house, but the former Empress spent, in all, no more than a month there in the course of a two-year period. Napoleon took it back and made ready an apartment for his son by Marie-Louise of Austria, the short-lived King of Rome or Napoleon II. The Emperor, now abdicated, was back here in the spring of 1815 on his return from Elba, leaving on June 12 for Waterloo. And it was at the Élysée, on June 22, 1815, that he signed his second abdication.

After Napoleon's departure, Czar Alexander I, a leader of the Allies against France, moved into the Élysée. There he received the Russian Baroness Julie de Krüdener, a pietistic "seer" with a considerable following. Alexander even considered her the inspiration behind his Holy Alliance, which he was about to offer for signature to Prince Metternich of Austria. Thus, when Alexander invited Metternich to dine with him at the Élysée, the only other guest was Baroness de Krüdener. Noting a fourth place set at table, Metternich, who understood it was to be a *souper à trois*, asked who the fourth guest was to be. The Baroness replied: "As always, Prince, a place is reserved for Jesus Christ."

At the restoration of the Bourbons, Louis XVIII assigned the Élysée to the Duc de Berry, his nephew and the presumed heir to the throne. When the Prince was assassinated at the Paris Opéra in 1820, the victim of an attempt to extinguish the Bourbon dynasty, his wife—Maria Carolina of Naples—became hysterical and cut off her long blond tresses, demanding that they be placed in her husband's coffin. Pregnant with the future pretender to the French throne—the Comte de Chambord—the Duchesse de Berry left the Élysée and moved in with the King at the Tuileries. There she would be worshiped by the poet Chateaubriand, whose loyalty to the Bourbons was never in doubt. "Madame," he told her, "your son is my King." Although titled Henri V, her son was never to rule, preferring to refuse the crown rather than reign under the *tricolore,* the flag of post-Revolutionary France.

In Louis-Philippe's time (1830–48) the Élysée went unoccupied and neglected save on rare occasions when visiting royalty were put up in the sumptuous apartments. But in the brief span of the Second Republic (1848–52), Louis-Napoleon, who had been elected President, decided to make the mansion his official residence. Apartments were renovated and the site enlarged by the purchase of the neighboring Hôtels de Castellane and de Sebastiani, both of which came down. A large glass porch appeared on the Élysée's courtyard side, masking the 18th-century façade,

Louis-Napoleon Bonaparte (1808–73)

while a more imposing street portal replaced the modest affair that had been there since the days of the Comte d'Évreux.

"The name of Napoleon is all we need in the way of a program," wrote the future Napoleon III. "It means, inside France, that order, authority, religion, and the welfare of the people will be maintained. Outside France, it stands for national dignity." He had already published a book, *Napoleonic Ideas*, making the most of his relationship to Napoleon I. While brooding over the future in the Élysée, he called on his cousin Princesse Mathilde, the daughter of the great Napoleon's brother Jérôme, King of Westphalia, to preside over his receptions. In less formal moments, the Prince-President counted on the company of Elizabeth Anne Howard, an Englishwoman who had lent him five million francs in the old days. This money would be returned, and she would be made Comtesse de Beauregard.

It was in the Salon d'Argent, the scene of Napoleon I's abdication, that the new defender of the Republic and his supporters organized the *coup d'état* of December 2, 1851. Said the Duc de Morny, who was deep in the plot: "I don't know what's going to happen. But if there is a clean sweep, rest assured that I will be on the side of the broom handle." That he was. As Napoleon III's half-brother, Morny won all the authority he could desire, which he exercised from the Hôtel Matignon on the Left Bank. The Second Empire became official in January 1852.

The Duchesse de Bourbon (1750–1822)

Half-adventurer, half-statesman, Napoleon III may never live down the scorn of Victor Hugo, but the Second Empire was more than a masquerade that ended in the disaster of the Franco-Prussian War. Driven by his uncle's heroic legend to play a military role for which he was not really suited—bloodshed on the battlefield actually sickened him—he also maintained that the Empire stood for peace. It did not, as everyone could tell when the French fought in the Crimea at the side of the English in 1853, or when the Emperor promoted a war for the liberation of Italy in 1859. A terrible mistake was Napoleon III's attempt to extend French imperialism to Mexico and there to create a throne with Maximilian of Austria seated upon it. This sorry drama had its dénouement in 1867 with death of Maximilian before Juarez' firing squad.

So much for the dark side of the Second Empire. Napoleon III did have something to his credit. This was a period of shrewd financial expansion, for agriculture greatly benefited from the Crédit Foncier, a mortgage bank established under the Emperor's auspices, and commercial banking received stimulation from the example of the great Crédit Lyonnais, with Henri Germain at the head. Louis-Napoleon must also be remembered as a city planner. Appointing Baron Haussmann prefect of the Seine, he gave Paris the parks for which it was starving and watched over the masterful plan that furnished the astounding boulevards. An architect manqué, the Emperor was willing to gamble on the age of iron, with the result that Baltard designed that compelling, now demolished monument, Les Halles, Paris' old central market.

For his Empress Napoleon III chose the beautiful Eugénie de Montijo, educated in the Convent of the Sacred Heart in the Hôtel de Biron. She and her mother stayed at the Élysée prior to the wedding in January 1853. The apartments were once again renovated, this time in a Second Empire pastiche inspired by what remained of the original 18th-century décor. During the ominous summer of 1867, the Emperor decided that the Élysée was the perfect place to house the various sovereigns who descended upon Paris for the great World's Fair.

During the Commune in the spring of 1871, a certain Monsieur de Gourlet, inspector of palaces, had the wit to seal the doors of the Élysée with the emblem of the revolutionists. This precaution saved the mansion from the arson that destroyed the three-hundred-year-old Tuileries Palace.

Largely because of the disarray among the monarchists—legitimists, Orleanists, and Bonapartists alike—France once again became a republic in 1871 and has retained that form of government ever since. With the Tuileries gone and the Louvre filled with the great state collections of art, the Élysée Palace assumed permanent status as the official residence of the French head of state, beginning with Adolphe Thiers. But as the elected representatives of a republic, Presidents could never indulge in the dramatic gestures so dear to the autocrats and monarchs of old. One, however—Sadi Carnot—must be remembered not only for his tragic assassination by an Italian anarchist (1894) but also for the additions he made to the Élysée—a huge Salle des Fêtes and a great glassed-in gallery that the French quickly christened *la cage aux singes* ("the monkey cage").

below: This room in the Élysée—originally the formal reception room of the Comte d'Évreux—was one of those redecorated by the Marquise de Pompadour in 1754. The paneling survives from that period, no doubt touched up by the enriching hands of the neo-Rococo decorators of the Second Empire. The gilded, damask-covered furniture matches the Savonnerie carpet of the Louis XV period.

opposite: The décor of the Murat Room dates from 1805–06, when it was designed by Percier and Fontaine, the official architects of the Napoleonic Empire. Originally the columns and pilasters framed four large landscape canvases, of which only two remain. One is a view of Rome's Castel Sant'Angelo, and the other a view of Benrath Castle. A modification made in 1855 shortened the room. On the mirrored wall hangs a copy of Ingres' masterful 1803 portrait of Napoleon as First Consul. The magnificent console table under the painting is an addition made by the Restoration monarchy in 1821. It has gilt-bronze fittings and plaques in Sèvres porcelain based upon paintings by Évariste Fragonard. The room remains a tribute to the monumental elegance of Neoclassical taste.

Hôtel de Païva

"Like virtue, vice has its degrees." Such is said to have been the inscription that the dramatist Émile Augier proposed for the astonishing house built for herself by one of the grandest *horizontales* of the Second Empire—the Marquise de Païva. The ideal location of this epigram would have been the pediment over the onyx-veneered grand staircase, itself a feature so overripe in the decorative wealth of its forms and materials as to constitute the perfect emblem of an age given over utterly to a parvenu appetite for opulence and ostentation. Remarkably, the title borne by the mistress of this house was real, but for all its high-sounding qualities, it could not conceal the eventful career of a notorious adventuress.

The Marquise de Païva was not born a peeress, but rather a Polish Jewess—one Thérèse Lachmann of humble origins—who first saw light in Moscow in 1819. Married very young to a French tailor named Villoing, she soon left him and made her way to Constantinople, where she passed herself off as one personage after another: the daughter of the Grand Duke Constantine, or an Indian Princess, or the superintendent of the Sultan's seraglio. About 1840 Thérèse turned up in Paris, where she met the famous pianist Henri Herz and immediately became his mistress. Through him she met some of the leading figures in the world of the arts, in particular Richard Wagner and the poet Théophile Gautier.

above: The voluptuous forms of the grand staircase in the Hôtel de Païva are either made of solid onyx or veneered in the same richly veined, translucent material. Standing vigil over the well is a statue of Dante by Aubé. In niches further up repose the images of Virgil, also by Cugniot, and of Petrarch by Barrias. A whole team of artists, including Carrier-Belleuse of Paris Opéra fame, contributed to the decoration of the hôtel. The most gifted of them was Jules Dalou, who carved the female bacchante over the fireplace in the dining room **(opposite).** Dalou also did the pair of faun caryatids, while Jacquemart carved the relief panel and the two lionesses.

Herz, however, found her too expensive to keep and saved himself by leaving France for the United States. Now Thérèse went through a difficult period. When Gautier called on her in rather squalid lodgings, she seemed desperate and spoke of suicide. Still, she resolved to try her luck once more, saying "If I fail, I am not the woman to earn my living as a seamstress. I mean to have the finest house in Paris some day. Mark my words!" To work out her plan, she came to an agreement with the famous dressmaker Camille, who supplied her with a series of dazzling gowns, all designed to set off the wearer's cold but commanding beauty. Thus

opposite: The main drawing room at the Hôtel de Païva, with its "enriched" interpretation of Renaissance-Baroque styles, is typical of the unrestrained lavishness favored in the age of Napoleon III. In this unbelievably overloaded setting, the red-marble fireplace has been embellished with gilt-bronze fittings. A relief at the center represents "The Dance of the Cupids," while the monumental female nudes by Delaplance symbolize Music and Harmony. Originally a great vase stood on the plinth between them. The woodwork—dark brown and gilded—frames wall sections covered in silk damask.   **right:** On the ceiling is Paul Baudry's painting *Day Driving Away Night,* for which the figure of Night is supposed to be a portrait of La Païva.

attired, she became a *femme fatale* and went forth to convert her personal assets into hard currency. Making no secret of her ambitions, she won the attention she coveted and gained the patronage of a succession of prominent, well-to-do men, including the Duc de Gramont, Lord Stanley, and the Duc de Guiche. Her stunning success prompted an observer to comment, once the great house on the Champs-Élysées had been built: "Only those who can afford it go there."

Having made her fortune and having learned of her husband's death, Thérèse decided in 1851 to marry a title and found an authentic one in the person of Albino Francisco, Marquis de Païva, cousin of the

Portuguese minister in Paris. The Marquis was deeply in debt, but that made him all the more pliable, therefore suitable: "I don't like husbands, but this one, it is true, is so little of a husband," she told Gautier. With such businesslike objectivity, Madame de Païva had no scruples about deserting her new spouse as soon as she met Count Henckel von Donnersmarck, a cousin of the Prussian chancellor Bismarck and the fabulously wealthy owner of copper mines in Silesia. Ten years her junior, the young Prussian fell under the power of La Païva, and soon the two were living together. Now, in 1851—the year of Louis-Napoleon's *coup d'état* that would make him Emperor of the French—La Païva found herself able to buy a piece of ground on the Champs-Élyées and to order from the architect Pierre Maugain "the finest house in Paris." It would contain precious marbles, gold, bronze, and mosaics in unheard-of profusion. Paul Baudry, the future decorator of the Paris Opéra, painted the ceiling in the main drawing room. Jules Dalou, best known as the creator of the great sculptural monument *The Triumph of the Republic* in the Place de la Nation, lent his considerable gifts to the decorative carving for the fireplace in the dining room. Moreover, he prepared relief compositions for the ceilings in the dining room and grand salon, a set of bronze reliefs for the library doors, and four console tables for the drawing room.

Once installed on the Champs-Élysées, La Païva gave dinners that immediately became famous for their rich and copious cuisine and for the luxury of the service. But all the guests were men. The women of Paris society, even those of little repute, avoided Madame de Païva, and, needless to say, she appeared on no guest list drawn up by the Empress Eugénie at the Tuileries. As for La Païva's true peers—the fashionable courtesans of the day—the Queen of the Champs-Élysées quite naturally saw them as rivals and refused to invite any. Her expensive dinners therefore lacked an essential element. The painter Delacroix noted in his *Journal*: "Dined at the home of the famous Comtesse de Païva. I dislike such unbridled luxury. An odd group of people. One comes away from such evenings with nothing to remember. One feels heavier the next day, that's all." Fortunately for the Marquise, not everyone shared Delacroix's opinion, and among her regular guests numbered many popular writers, in addition to such serious-minded intellectuals as Sainte-Beuve, Taine, and Renan.

In 1871 La Païva contrived to secure a papal annulment of her marriage with the Marquis, who a year later, sorely beset by his creditors, blew his brains out after a final all-night spree in Paris. Now the courtesan and her German Count could marry in a full-scale Church ceremony. Soon afterwards, von Donnersmarck was appointed governor of Alsace-Lorraine, the eastern provinces France had lost to Germany at the close of the Franco-Prussian War. La Païva had become a great lady indeed. But in 1879 she and her husband suddenly left Paris and were never again seen on French soil.

La Païva died in 1884 at Neudeck, Silesia, in a château built to her palatial taste by the French architect Hector Lefuel, who had remodeled the Louvre for Napoleon III. Thus liberated from his *femme fatale*, Count von Donnersmarck shortly thereafter took a second wife, this time a young woman of the highest German aristocracy, who gave him many children. In 1893 he sold La Païva's Paris house to a Berlin banker. This proprietor then leased it to Monsieur Cubat, former head chef to Czar Alexander II, who converted the place into a luxurious restaurant, which, however, was not a success. Emptied of its original furniture, a few pieces of which can be seen in the Musée des Arts Decoratifs, the Hôtel de Païva is now occupied by the Traveller's Club.

Monceau
The Chaussée-d'Antin
Neuilly

Hôtel Nissim de Camondo
Hôtel de la Princesse Mathilde
Hôtel de Bourrienne
La Folie Saint-James

At the Hôtel Nissim de Camondo, one
lacquered ebony cabinet of a pair bearing the stamp
of the cabinetmaker Adam Weisweiler

Hôtel Nissim de Camondo

above: Built in 1911–14 from plans by Sargent, the Hôtel de Nissim de Camondo, with its lightly concave façade, is a remarkably skilled and sensitive evocation of the Louis XVI style of Gabriel in the Petit Trianon.   **opposite:** In the vestibule the architect made the most of mirror effects, so that here is reflected the grand staircase with its magnificent wrought-iron handrail. The shell fountain, which seems all the more Baroque for its red marble material and its lead dolphin and green-painted reeds, came from the Château de Saint-Prix, an estate in the Montmórency Forest owned by another famous collector, Baron Léopold Double.

"Desiring to perpetuate the memory of my father, the Comte Nissim de Camondo, and that of my unfortunate son, the aviator Lieutenant Nissim de Camondo, shot down in combat on September 5, 1917, I bequeath to the Museum of Decorative Arts my house such as it may consist of at the time of my death. To my house shall be given the name of Nissim de Camondo, the name of my son for whom this house and its collections were intended. It is my intention, in bequeathing to the state my house and the collections it contains, that the work to which I have applied myself, that of reconstituting an artistic home of the 18th century, shall be preserved in its entirety. The purpose of this reconstitution should be to preserve in France, in a setting peculiarly appropriate to them, the finest objects that I have been able to find of that decorative art which was one of the glories of France during the period that I have loved above all others."

Such were the attitudes and aspirations, expressed in his own words, of the Comte Moïse de Camondo (1860–1935) when this great financial magnate set about to form a fabulous collection of 18th-century French decorative arts, to house it in an hôtel modeled upon Gabriel's Petit Trianon at Versailles, and then to transform the whole into the Musée Nissim de Camondo. Count Moïse belonged to a wealthy family of Jewish bankers long resident in Constantinople, before they moved to Paris in the mid-19th century. There his father, the first Comte Nissim de Camondo, and his uncle, Count Abraham, commissioned two neighboring houses at 61 and 63 Rue de Monceau. This was the forested, game-rich area, then on the outskirts of Paris, that the Duc d'Orléans—head of the junior branch of the French royal family and known to history as the Philippe-Égalité of the Revolution and the father of King Louis-Philippe

(r. 1830–48)—had caused to be transformed into his own private garden in 1778, just eleven years before the storming of the Bastille. And it was an English garden that the Duc d'Orléans ordered, the finest, it turned out, ever to exist in France. In 1852, after the fall of the Orleanist regime of Louis-Philippe, the financier Pereire took over the park and parceled up much of it for the construction of *hôtels de luxe*, while the engineer Alphand adapted what remained for use as a public park, still in the English manner and still studded with a number of the original "follies." Along its perimeters rose the finest houses to be built in Paris during the

Second Empire, most of them gloriously ostentatious as only the age of Napoleon III could have tolerated. In 1911–14 Moïse de Camondo replaced his father's grandiose mansion with the elegant Louis XVI re-creation by Sargent, best known in the United States as the collaborator with Horace Trumbauer on the New York town house-gallery of Duveen Brothers. The entire structure was designed about the magnificent collections that Count Moïse had brought together.

In the holocaust of World War II, tragedy once again struck the Camondo family, which became extinct when Madame Léon Reinach, Count Moïse's daughter, and all her family perished at Auschwitz:

below: The large study in the Hôtel Nissim de Camondo is graced by paneling that dates partly from the 18th century. The Aubusson tapestries set into the woodwork illustrate the *Fables* of La Fontaine and were woven from designs by Oudry. In front of the fireplace stand a pair of *voyueses,* those *prie-Dieu* chairs designed to enable ladies to kneel while watching card games. Created by Séné, they came from the collection of Madame Élisabeth, Louis XVI's sister, at the Château de Montreuil. Leleu produced the two large cabinets that flank the fireplace. On top of the mahogany, bronze-fitted rolltop desk stand three vases of Niederwiller faience made about 1770–95. The armchair in front of the desk is of gilt wood, upholstered on the inside with leather and with caning on the outside. **opposite:** The lacquered, bronze embellished corner cupboard on the stair landing is one of a pair attributed to B.V.R.B. (Bernard van Risenburgh).

above: The silver holloware collected by Comte Moise de Camondo originally formed part of an extensive dinner service made in 1770–71 by the French master Jacques Roettiers. Here displayed in the dining room, in combination with a set of Sèvres porcelain, the service was a present from the Catherine the Great to her favorite, Prince Gregory Orlov.   **opposite:** The Huet Room is named for the artist J. B. Huet, who in 1776 painted the pastoral scenes that now decorate these walls in the Hôtel Nissim de Camondo. The matched cabinets on either side of the door belonged to the Duc de Penthièvre and came from the Château de Bizy. The pair of *vermeil,* or "silver-gilt," candlesticks in the foreground, made by T. F. Germain and dated 1762, bear the arms of Madame de Pompadour.

The grand salon at the Hôtel Nissim de Camondo is paneled with Louis XVI woodwork from a town house originally in the Rue Royale. Here have been assembled the finest pieces of furniture in the Camondo collection: a small desk by Carlin inlaid with plaques of Sèvres porcelain **(opposite above)**; a commode by Riesener **(opposite below)**; and **(below)** a Savonnerie carpet under a small gilt-bronze pedestal table attributed to Thomire and a set of chairs and settees upholstered in Aubusson tapestry and signed by Jacob. The Beauvais tapestry on the wall belongs to a series on the theme of Italian festivals.

Hôtel de la Princesse Mathilde

For those who think of the Second Empire as an era almost self-parodying in its love of lush and overscaled grandeur, the Hôtel de la Princesse Mathilde will surely come as a surprise. But in this modest house, in a newly created, *grand bourgeois* neighborhood far from the traditional bastions of aristocratic Paris, unfolded the enduring love of two figures generally thought to be so representative of the *faux papiers* Second Empire as to be incapable of pure or admirable intentions. The mistress of the house was none other than Princess Mathilde, daughter of Catherine of Württenberg and Jérôme Bonaparte, Napoleon I's youngest brother and the dethroned King of Westphalia. Without money of her own and in retreat from a brutal marriage, to the Russian Count Anatole Demidov, Prince of San Donato, Princess Mathilde found refuge in the Rue de Courcelles and solace in a long and gratifying liaison with Count de Nieuwerkerke, Napoleon III's Minister of Fine Arts and the sworn enemy of innovation, at a time when France was experiencing a burst of artistic creativity virtually unparalleled in human history. Hard as it is to like anyone who made life difficult for Courbet, Manet, Monet, Renoir, and Cézanne, the dignity that Princess Mathilde and Count de Nieuwerkerke brought to one another ultimately succeeds in commanding a good measure of respect.

Titled but undowered, Princess Mathilde had been married at a very young age, to create an alliance with a family only recently ennobled by the Czar but fabulously rich from the manufacture of arms (which had

In the vestibule of the *premier étage* (second floor) a pair of Louis XVI armchairs flank a handsome commode in the style of Cressent.

In the large drawing room of the Hôtel de la Princesse Mathilde the color of the damask on the walls was inspired by the cerise satin worn by the Baroness James de Rothschild in her 1842–48 portrait by Ingres **(below).** (See the color view on page 259.) This masterwork now hangs in the Hôtel Lambert (see page 79). The wall covering makes a lustrous background for a superb collection of period furniture and objets d'art. The finest of the pieces are the Louis XV armchairs and settees. Something rare is the small lacquered, Sèvres-inlaid table in the foreground **(opposite).** A similar table now in the Louvre bears the stamp of Bernard van Risenburgh.

been used against the Princess' uncle, Napoleon I). Count Demidov possessed a splendid palace in Florence, the Villa San Donato, and much personal charm. Toward his wife, however, he seemed unable to be anything but odious. Although maniacally jealous of her, he maintained a lover of his own and flaunted her before his wife and the world at large. To humiliate Mathilde he would keep her waiting in a carriage for hours,

opposite: In the clear-finished woodwork of the library at the Hôtel de la Princesse Mathilde are glass-enclosed shelves containing priceless objects worked in silver and gold by German and Italian masters of the 16th and 17th centuries.
above: In an adjacent parlor both the divan and the floor are covered in flower-patterned tapestry. The cabinet above the divan has been veneered in satinwood and adorned with bronze fittings in the style of Cressent.

257

while he was upstairs holding *un rendez-vous d'affaires* in a house known to be occupied by his mistress. After Waterloo, the situation of the Bonapartes was such that Jérôme had to depend upon his son-in-law for an income. When this proved inadequate, Mathilde went to Demidov and requested a supplement, which he took a mean delight in refusing. After much futile pleading, the Princess collapsed in tears, whereupon her husband rang for a footman. "There," he said, pointing to Mathilde, "you see the niece of the great Napoleon down on her knees begging me for money to give to her father." On another occasion, at a fancy dress ball in the Villa San Donato, the Princess appeared beautifully attired as Diana, only to find her husband parading about with his mistress on his arm. He never left this lady's side all evening, and when Mathilde dared to say a word about it, he slapped her in front of all the guests. This scandal reached the ears of Czar Nicholas I, who told her: "You don't know what a beast you have married." "Your Majesty," she answered, "is most ungenerous in speaking of the man who is my husband." "My poor child, you will one day realize the truth of what I've said, and then you will come to me for help. You may always rely on my support." Princess Mathilde did not forget this advice and finally applied to the Czar for the dissolution of her marriage. Nicolas kept his word, not only annulling the marriage and forbidding Demidov to leave Russia until further notice, but also compelling him to pay the Princess a yearly pension of 200,000 gold francs, 40,000 of which was for the maintenance of King Jérôme. Mathilde was also allowed to keep one-half of the Demidov diamonds, whose value was estimated at more than a million francs.

Having survived her years of suffering, Princess Mathilde found love at the same time that she won her liberty. And the decorum with which she and Nieuwerkerke behaved permitted them to be received as if they were a proper couple. Arsène Houssaye wrote: "We congratulate the Princess on having passed a 'new church' [*nieuwerkerke* in Dutch] wearing a crown of orange blossoms. How many women have been saved from a debasing marriage by love? The Princess was beautiful, spirited, and charming, and she possessed a marvelous grace of speech on every subject. Aristocratic, the daughter of a King, the bearing of an Empress—to know her was to like her."

At 10 Rue de Courcelles, then at number 24 in the same street, and finally, after the fall of the Second Empire, in the nearby Rue de Berri, Princess Mathilde kept a salon that became one of the most celebrated in the second half of the 19th century. There could be found the politicians Thiers, Prévost-Paradol, Émile Ollivier; the writers Taine, Renan, Flaubert, Gautier, the Goncourts, the Dumas, Augier, and About; also the great rival painters Ingres and Delacroix. But no closer could the Princess move toward the artistic avant-garde, for Nieuwerkerke, although a bit of a sculptor in his own right, claimed to have no use for "the painting of democrats, of those who don't change their linen, and who want to put themselves over on men of the world." Considering himself very much a man of the world, Nieuwerkerke did not want to be made fun of, which, to those who could not understand, the radical innovators appeared to be doing. For his unperceptiveness and ruthless denial of official support for Manet and his followers, the world concerned about the modernist movement in art has never forgiven either Nieuwerkerke or Princess Mathilde.

After changing hands several times, the Hôtel de la Princesse Mathilde became the residence of Baron Guy de Rothschild, whose great-grandmother Betty (Baroness James de Rothschild) surveyed the salon, from her image in the portrait by Ingres, until the Rothschilds moved to the Hôtel Lambert, taking the painting with them (see page 79).

Princess Mathilde (1820–1904)

opposite: In this plate appears the daring cerise of the wall damask in the large drawing room of the Hôtel de la Princesse Mathilde (see also pages 254–255.) The polychrome marble fireplace is a delicate work of the Louis XV period. Like the candelabra and the bronze-mounted Chinese porcelain it supports, the andirons and the bracket lamps are all period pieces.

Hôtel de Bourrienne

opposite: The dining room in the Hôtel de Bourrienne survives as one of the most perfect examples known of the Directory style, which at the time was referred to as the "Etruscan manner," for its relatively archaeological and severe Neoclassicism. It led out of the Louis XVI style and to the Empire style, before this became overlaid, profuse, and somewhat overscaled. The slender, simplified Corinthian colonnade gives access to a room decorated with mirrors flanked by tall panels stuccoed in a relief pattern inspired by the 18th-century findings at Pompeii.
above: The décor of the plain façade on the hôtel's garden side is limited to four figural reliefs placed between the main bays of the central pavilion. They symbolize Victory.

Juliette Récamier—painted by David and Gérard, adored by Madame de Staël, and a famously perceptive listener—will forever reign as the most beautiful woman in France at the dawn of the 19th century, but in her time even this paragon had to share the world with other beauties. One of these was Madame Hamelin, who could easily have posed as a *merveilleuse*, or "elegant lady," of the Directory era (1795–99), when France was on the verge of being ruled by three Consuls headed by Napoleon. The interiors of the Hôtel de Bourrienne, where Madame Hamelin resided from 1792 to 1801, are exceptional demonstrations of the Directory style, a Neoclassical mode lighter than the Empire style but clearly leading to it. Here are arabesques and bas-reliefs that are immortal in the eyes of anyone concerned with that climactic moment in the decorative arts— the age of Napoleon. The name of the architect of the Hôtel de Bourrienne, begun in 1787 for Madame de Bazin de Dampierre, who sold it in 1792 to Madame Hamelin's father, has not come down to us, but we know that Madame Hamelin had it decorated by François-Joseph Bélanger, the man responsible for the Folie Saint-James (see pages 266–272).

Like Joséphine, Napoleon's first wife, Madame Hamelin possessed the exotic qualities of the Creole, and she knew how to set them off with gowns made of the lightest, most clinging muslin. Too, she had the daring and the panache to launch fashions, such as the shawl and the waltz. The Duchesse d'Abrantès, the wife of Napoleon's General Junot, depicts Madame Hamelin as "lively and laughter-loving, and given to pranks— like a cat with rather long claws." The claws could also be sharp, even in regard to Madame Récamier. One evening the latter left a ball escorted by *le beau* Montrond, a fop in whom Madame Hamelin considered she had proprietary rights. Following in her own carriage, she caught up with the couple and began screaming: "Help! Help! The wretched woman in that carriage is running away with my husband!" Madame Récamier, somewhat alarmed, thrust her head through the window. "Oh, Madame," cried La Hamelin, "is it you? I'm sorry! I've made a mistake!" Indeed it was a mistake to have bothered, for by then Madame Récamier's interests lay elsewhere, mainly in Lucien Bonaparte.

In 1801 Madame Hamelin sold the house to Louis-Antoine Fauvelet de Bourrienne, a schoolmate of Napoleon who in 1796 lent him the money to travel to Italy, where he took command of the French army. In return, Napoleon made Fauvelet his private secretary and then, in 1804, sent him on a special mission to Hamburg. However, Bourrienne mismanaged his affairs and got into debt. And in 1814 he deserted Napoleon to make his peace with the Bourbons. Under Louis XVIII he got the job of Prefect of Police. Later Fauvelet's mind gave way, and he had to withdraw from public life, dying in Caen in 1834.

By 1886 the Hôtel de Bourrienne had passed to Charles Tulen de Berny, a type-founder who set up his workshops in the garden. This was a humble moment. A better time came in our own generation, when Jean Peignot, founder of the Friends of Historic Houses, redeemed and restored the hôtel both inside and out.

opposite: In the main salon of the Hôtel de Bourrienne the motifs of the painted decorations, the reliefs, and the carved architectural enframements have the severe, almost archaeological classicism typical of the Directory. The "cameos," the arabesques, and the figures draped *à l'antique*, the candelabra, vases, and palmettes all had their inspiration in the recent findings at Pompeii and Herculaneum **(see also pages 264–265).** The décor of the bedroom **(above left)** and the bathroom **(above right)** was executed somewhat later, at the very end of the 18th century, and thus approaches the Empire taste for a heavier, more spectacular Neoclassicism. The image of the swan, with its spare but elegant and erotic silhouette, would become almost ubiquitous in the Empire period.

The Duchesse d'Abrantès (1785–1838)

La Folie Saint-James

Morally, he may not have been impeccable, but his talent was undeniable. This perhaps is the quickest way to introduce François-Joseph Bélanger, the architect of the hôtel called La Folie Saint-James. Begun in 1775 and completed five years later, the Folie lies only a step away from the Pont de Neuilly, which leads to the Bois de Boulogne. Thus, within walking distance of the Folie Saint-James can be found Bélanger's most famous achievement, the exquisite jewellike Château de Bagatelle, for which the Bois de Boulogne served as park. Built in only sixty-four days, Bagatelle was finished by November 26, 1777—just in time for the owner, the Comte d'Artois, Louis XVI's younger brother, to win the bet he made with Marie-Antoinette that he could move in so soon. Thomas Jefferson, who missed no architecture worth seeing in the years when he was the American minister at the French court, made a point of inspecting Bagatelle. He realized, as did Bélanger, that the royal Prince was a client

On its garden façade the Folie Saint-James is entered by way of a graceful portico supported by slender, faceted, spiral columns. The arcade resting upon columns seems more akin to the Early Italian Renaissance than to the French Neoclassical style, which, however, is dominant in the sphinxes at the bottom of the steps, in the winged Victories in the spandrels, and in the palmette friezes. Bélanger, who built the house in 1775–80, here made formal departures that heralded the Directory style of 1793–1804.

worth cultivating. In six years Artois spent 4,200,000 *livres* on architecture, and thus was running three years behind on the annual income promised his architect. In 1824, when the Comte d'Artois, at age sixty-seven, came to the throne as Charles X, he was still elegant and charming—and too much the product of the *ancien régime* to prevent the revolution of 1830 that sent him into exile, forever ending the Bourbon dynasty of France.

If Bélanger continued to work for his royal patron even when not paid, it was because he had long since learned to be patient. In 1765, after failing to win the coveted Prix de Rome, Bélanger went off to England for two years. There he worked for Lord Shelbourne at Bowood, while also studying the great gardens of Lord Cobham at Stowe. This prepared him, once he returned to his native country, to capitalize on the anglomania that swept France in the final years of Louis XV's reign. Besides giving advice to the Prince de Ligne about his gardens at Beloeil in Flanders, he made an indelible impression on Jean-Joseph Laborde, the banker who was planning to do great things at Méréville, his country house near Étampes. At Méréville, Bélanger worked in the gardens by the side of Hubert Robert, the great Rococo painter of decorative and idyllic landscapes. Together the artists filled the gardens with *fabriques*, those "follies," caprices, or inventions formed in imitation of Greek tem-

opposite: The façade on the courtyard at the Folie Saint-James echoes the general design of the garden front, except that here the Ionic portico with its massive, smooth columns replaces the slender, faceted grace of the garden porch. The portico, the pediment, the quoins, the moldings, and the cameo medallions are all creamy white and set off against the background pink of the stucco wall.

below: Now much reduced in size, the garden à *l'anglaise* behind the house was originally strewn with a variety of *fabriques*, those "follies" or sham Greek temples, Chinese pagodas, and Dutch mills designed to create a Romantic and picturesque effect. Fortunately, the largest and the most interesting has survived—the grotto. Built of boulders brought from the Fontainebleau Forest and set behind an artificial lake, the grotto is entered through a small pseudoantique temple inspired by the great Doric monuments of Paestum.

ples, Chinese pagodas, or Dutch mills and designed to make an English style garden seem even more picturesque.

The fame enjoyed by Bélanger under the *ancien régime*, while great, does not seem to have helped him much in later years. But in 1808 he got the chance to redo the wooden dome of the Halle au Blé ("Grain Market") that had recently been destroyed by fire. Using cast-iron ribs tied by wrought-iron rings, he constructed the first iron dome in history. This has vanished, but not before giving Bélanger a good claim to consideration as a modern architect. He was not quite so inventive at the Folie Saint-James, even though the columns carrying arches on the garden side provided an ancient Roman as well as a Renaissance motif—an idea that would soon become extremely popular, as can be seen in the front porch and veranda architecture of Victorian America.

The Folie Saint-James, we are told, was commissioned when Monsieur Baudard de Vaudésir, Baron de Saint-Gemmes (which became Saint-James at the height of the anglomania epidemic), found himself sleepless over the tour de force of Bagatelle. To cure his affliction, he commissioned the Folie. To do this, Saint-James had had his more practical moments, for while serving as treasurer to the navy, he built a fortune by investing in silk mills and fire extinguishers. But a much greater folly than the Paris hôtel was his decision to lend 800,000 *livres* to the jewelers who produced the notorious diamond necklace that figured in the fraud worked upon Marie-Antoinette by the vainglorious Cardinal Louis de Rohan. Driven into bankruptcy and imprisoned, Saint-James died on his release in 1787 of grief and hurt pride.

For the gardens at the Folie, Saint-James ordered a number of follies or *fabriques*, only a few of which have survived. One of these—the grotto—became famous for the enormous cost and effort required to bring the huge rocks used in it all the way from Fontainebleau Forest. One day, it is said, Louis XVI was returning from the hunt when he found himself blocked in the road by a team of forty horses pulling a dray laden with one colossal, cyclopian boulder. Curious about the bizarre convoy, the King learned that it was destined for the English gardens of Monsieur de Saint-James. This creation continued to pull the royal family up short, for when the Comte d'Artois, Bagatelle's builder, saw the finished grotto, he declared: "I would like to divert onto my own property the stream of gold that flows from that enormous rock."

In the wake of the Revolution the Folie Saint-James was acquired by the banker Hainguerlot, who in 1800 rented it to Lucien Bonaparte. Napoleon's brother had just lost his wife and had been joined by his sister, Elisa Baciocchi, the future Grand Duchess of Tuscany.

By 1808 the tenant of the Folie was Laure Junot, Duchesse d'Abrantès, who in her *Mémoires* made a detailed account of an idyll she had once shared with the great Austrian statesman Metternich, then ambassador to Paris. The scene was the Folie Saint-James. Affronted by her husband's open affair with Caroline Murat, Napoleon's sister, the Duchesse d'Abrantès did what she could to console herself. Thus, in the summer of 1808 she mounted a production of Marivaux's *Marriage of Figaro*, with herself in the lead role of Rosina. "I overdid myself," she wrote. "The exhaustion of that evening had revived the feeling of inner disquiet that had bothered me sometime before. I took off my costume, and, putting on a big muslin robe, I went down into my little garden to breathe in the fragrance of my beautiful flowers. . . . When I got to the grotto the interior was not altogether dark, thanks to an opening in the vault through which moonlight could pass. But the shadows began to frighten me when I thought I heard a noise. I went back into the garden and . . . began to quicken my step, only to feel faint as suddenly there was the

The vestibule at the Folie Saint-James **(see also page 272)** is decorated in *trompe l'oeil* painting with architectural elements, sculpture, and vases. This type of ornamentation was often used for such spaces in the 17th and 18th centuries. In the Neoclassical setting here the wrought-iron balustrade from the Rococo, Louis XV period comes as a surprise. It must have been taken from another house and installed later.

sound of someone following me. I would certainly have fainted if the voice that now fell upon my ears had not been a familiar one. Then all of a sudden there I was collapsed in the arms of Monsieur de Metternich. . . . 'Oh, you are crying,' he said, 'and you allow me to suffer!' " Very quickly, Laure avowed, "she no longer knew what was happening to her." She discovered herself back in the grotto, having "made a 'mistake' that [she] would want to expiate with tears of blood." When this was written the Duchesse d'Abrantès was having to live as best she could by her pen. Meanwhile, Metternich had become the all-powerful Chancellor of the Austrian Empire.

A charming adornment of the garden at the Folie Saint-James is a small circular temple whose Tuscan peristyle and cupola shelter a sculptural Venus and Cupid.

From 1833 to 1851, the Folie belonged to a certain Bénazet, the operator of no less than seven gambling halls. "Gambling," said Bénazet, "is the kind of social leprosy that can only be cured by time and by one step at a time. Rushing matters will do no good at all and only cause new outbreaks of the evil."

During the summer of 1842 Bénazet let the Folie to a much-matured Juliette Récamier, who had Chateaubriand among her guests. In 1844 Dr. Pinel, nephew of the famous specialist in mental disorders, used the Folie as a psychiatric clinic. Later, his son-in-law, Dr. Sémelaigne, as head of the clinic, would treat the troubled painter Toulouse-Lautrec, committed to care by his mother.

Today the Folie Saint-James houses the Institut de Jeunes Filles de Neuilly.

Index

Hôtel d'Aumont

Asterisks refer to houses described in the book, at the pages indicated.

* HÔTEL DES AMBASSADEURS
DE HOLLANDE
47, rue Vieille-du-Temple (see page 56)

HÔTEL AMELOT DE GOURNAY
1, rue Saint-Dominique

Built in 1712, this is one of Germain Boffrand's most original creations. The main courtyard is oval-shaped. The principal building, adorned with pilasters, has been given an inward curve, at each end of which are low horseshoe wings. The house passed from the Amelot family to the Princes de Tingry, then to the Comte de Guerchy, French Ambassador in London, who let it to the parents of Talleyrand. Privately owned.

* THE ARSENAL
1, rue de Sully (see page 48)

HÔTEL D'AUMONT
10, place de la Concorde

Now the Hôtel Crillon, it occupies part of the façade of the building that forms a pair with the Ministère de la Marine ("Navel Ministry"), both built by Jacques-Ange Gabriel. The apartments were magnificently decorated by Pâris for the Duc d'Aumont. The woodwork of the main drawing room and the dining room, replaced by plaster copies, was removed in the early 20th century and reinstalled in the Hôtel de La Tour d'Auvergne, 2, avenue de La Motte-Picquet, now the Chilian Embassy.

HÔTEL D'AUMONT
7, rue de Jouy

It takes its name from the Ducs d'Aumont, a family of great noblemen and keen collectors who lived there from 1648 to 1742. The house was built in the 1640s by Louis Le Vau for Michel Scarron, uncle of Madame de Maintenon's future husband and father of Catherine Scarron who in 1629 had married the Marquis de Villequier, created Duc d'Aumont in 1665. For him, the house was remodeled by François Mansart and the apartments were magnificently decorated. Of those decorations, little now remains. Purchased by the City of Paris in 1935 and recently restored, the Hôtel d'Aumont houses the Tribunal Administratif de la Seine.

* HÔTEL D'AVARAY
85, rue de Grenelle (see page 172)

BAGATELLE
Bois de Boulogne

This charming "folly" was built in 1778 by the architect Bélanger, who accomplished the task in days, doing so for the Comte d'Artois, the future Charles X, as the result of a bet the latter had made with his sister-in-law, Queen Marie-Antoinette. In the 19th century it belonged to Sir Richard Wallace, who disfigured it by raising the height of the building in a neo-Louis XVI style. The drawing rooms still have their admirable paneling in the Pompeiian style.

HÔTEL DE BAUFFREMONT
87, rue de Grenelle

Built in 1721–36 for the Comte d'Ourouër, the house was occupied by the Comte d'Albert, made Prince of Grimbergen in 1729 by the Elector of Bavaria. It later belonged to the Marquis de Brunoy; to the Comtesse de Boisgelin, canoness of Remiremont; and in the 19th century to the Princes-Ducs de Bauffremont, who leased the first floor to Prince Metternich while he was Austrian Ambassador in Paris. Owned by Monsieur Bemberg.

* HÔTEL DE BEAUHARNAIS
78, rue de Lille (see page 136)

Bagatelle

HÔTEL DE BEAUVAIS
68, rue François-Miron

Built for Catherine de Beauvais, The lady's maid and confidant to whom Anne of Austria gave the delicate task of sexually initiating her son, Louis XIV, when he was sixteen. Catherine's cleverness and gift for intrigue having enabled her to accumulate a considerable fortune, she had this house built for herself in 1658 by Antoine Lepautre. Unfortunately, it was much remodeled in the 19th century. From its balconies, in 1660, the Queen Mother (Anne of Austria), the Queen of England, and Cardinal Mazarin watched the triumphal entry into Paris of Louis XIV and his young Spanish wife, Marie-Thérèse.

* HÔTEL DE BESENVAL
142, rue de Grenelle (see page 188)

* HÔTEL DE BIRON
77, rue de Varenne (see page 178)

* HÔTEL DE BOISGELIN
47, rue de Varenne (see page 128)

HÔTEL BONY
32, rue de Trévise

Built in 1826 by the architect Bony. Both in its external design and in its interior decoration, it is the finest example of a Paris town house in the Restoration style. Long left in a sorry state of neglect, the house is soon to be repaired and restored.

HÔTEL BOTTEREL-QUINTIN
44, rue des Petites-Ecuries

Built in 1780 by Pérard de Montreuil for the Intendant de La Corée, it was purchased in 1785 by the Comte de Botterel-Quintin, who had it entirely redecorated, perhaps to the designs of Bélanger. Although the main drawing room has lost its fireplace and its landscape paintings by Hubert Robert, the dining room remains a beautiful example of the Directory style, with its stucco columns, arabesque panels, and ceiling frieze attributed to Prud'hon. The charming Pompeiian decoration of the staircase is slightly later in date. Privately owned.

HÔTEL DE BOUILLON
17, quai Malaquais

It owes its name to one of Mazarin's nieces, Marie-Anne Mancini, Duchesse de Bouillon and patroness of La Fontaine, an intelligent and cultivated woman who led a loose life. Built in 1640 by François Mansart, the house was remodeled in 1741. The ground-floor apartments still have part of the decoration carried out in 1808 for Stéphanie Tascher de La Pagerie, Duchesse d'Arenberg. Owned by the École des Beaux-Arts.

Hôtel de Beauvais

HÔTEL DE BOURBON-CONDÉ
12, rue Monsieur

This whole neighborhood was built up by A. T. Brongniart, who put up this house in 1781 for Mademoiselle de Bourbon, daughter of the Prince de Condé. As Abbess of Remiremont, she founded in 1816 an order of Benedictine nuns called the Order of the Perpetual Adoration of the Holy Sacrament. The house has lost the bas-reliefs by Clodion which once adorned the courtyard, but still has its beautiful interior décor. Owned by the Institut Privé Rue Monsieur.

*HÔTEL DE BOURRIENNE
58, rue d'Hauteville (see page 260)

HÔTEL DE BRANCAS
6, rue de Tournon

Built in the early 18th century by Bullet for Jean-Baptiste Terrat, chancellor of the Regent. It was acquired in 1763 by the Duc de Brancas, whose son had a stormy laison with the famous actress and opera singer Sophie Arnould. Privately owned.

*HÔTEL DE BRIENNE
14, rue Saint-Dominique (see page 102)

*HÔTEL CARNAVALET
23, rue de Sévigné (see page 38)

HÔTEL DE CASTRIES
72, rue de Varenne

Built in 1696, it was acquired in 1708 by the Marquis de Castries and remained in his family until 1866. In November 1790, after a duel between the Comte Charles de Lameth, who had espoused the revolutionary cause, and the first Duc de Castries, who stood out against it, the house was sacked by the mob. The apartments still have most of their superb woodwork, dating to about 1743. The ground floor is occupied today by a private tenant, while on the upper floor are the offices of a governmental ministry.

HÔTEL DE CHÂLONS-LUXEMBOURG
16, rue Geoffroy-L'Anier

This charming brick-and-stone town house in the Louis XIII style was built in 1600–10 for Monsieur de La Boderie, French Ambassador to England. It was later occupied by the Châlons family, then by the Béon-Luxembourg family. It now houses the Fondation des Bourses Zelidja.

HÔTEL DE CHANALEILLES
2, rue de Chanaleilles

A "folly" built about 1770 and acquired in 1799 by the famous Madame Tallien, later Princesse de Chimay. It was subsequently owned by the Marquis de Chanaleilles and, since 1956, by Mr. Stavros Niarchos, who has restored it admirably and there installed his extensive collection.

HÔTEL DE CHAROLAIS
99, rue de Grenelle

Built in 1700–04 by Lassurance. The elegant façades are intact, but in the apartments nothing remains of the original décor. Among its occupants were Philippe d'Orléans-Longueville, Marquis de Rothelin; Mademoiselle de Charolais, daughter of the Duc de Bourbon and Mademoiselle de Nantes; and, under the First Empire, Lucien Bonaparte. From 1827 to 1860 it housed the Ministry of the Interior (Casimir Perier died there of cholera in 1832); then, after 1861, the Austrian Embassy. Here, in 1867, Princess Metternich gave a splendid fête for Napoleon III and the Empress Eugénie. It is now occupied by the Ministère du Commerce ("Ministry of Trade").

*HÔTEL DE CHÂROST
39, rue du Faubourg-Saint-Honoré (see page 208)

*HÔTEL DU CHÂTELET
127, rue de Grenelle (see page 124)

HÔTEL DE CHAULNES
9, place des Vosges

Built in 1607 by Pierre Fougue, Sieur Descures, and sold by his daughter in 1644 to the Duc de Chaulnes. There the Duchesse de Chaulnes twice received Anne of Austria and her retinue. Becoming a widow, the Duchess made over the house to her son, the second Duc de Chaulnes, governor of Brittany, who had it lavishly decorated and lived there in high style. Madame de Sévigné, a close friend of the family, describes a dinner there at which she "ate like a devil and drank like a fish." Sold in 1701 to Jean-Aimar de Nicolai, the house passed to his son who redecorated it at the end of the 18th century. The actress Rachel had an apartment, in the house, where her funeral service was held in 1858. Owned by the Académie d'Architecture.

HÔTEL DE CLERMONT-TONNERRE
118–120, rue du Bac

Actually a twin pair of houses, one of which was occupied by a member of the Clermont-Tonnerre family in the 18th century. Chateaubriand lived on the ground floor of No. 120 from 1838 until his death in 1848, there dictating his autobiography (*Mémoires d'outre-tombe*). Privately owned.

HÔTEL DE CLUNY
6, place Painlevé

Now the Musée de Cluny, the house was built at the end of the 15th century to the order of Jean III de Bourbon, Abbot of Cluny (in Burgundy). It was later placed at the disposal of the French Kings, who used it to house distinguished guests, like Mary Tudor, widow of Louis XII, and James V of Scotland. There in 1833 the archaeologist Alexandre du Sommerard installed his collections, which, together with the house, were bought by the government in 1843.

THE COMMUNAUTÉ SAINTE-AURE
27, rue Lhomond

This charming Louis XV house was occupied in the 18th century by a religious community, a sisterhood, where the future Madame du Barry was educated. It has been admirably restored by its present owner, the architect Laprade.

HÔTEL DE MADEMOISELLE
DUCHESNOIS
3, rue de la Tour-des-Dames

Like the neighboring Hôtel de Talma and Hôtel de Mademoiselle Mars, this house was built in 1820 to the designs of Constantin, a pupil of Percier and Fontaine. The façades, rounded on the courtyard side and decorated with a loggia on the garden side, are in an elegant Neoclassical style. Privately owned.

Hôtel de Bourbon-Condé

Hôtel de Chanaleilles

Hôtel de Chaulnes

Hôtel de Cluny

Hôtel d'Évreux

Hôtel d'Évreux
19, place Vendôme

Built in 1708 by Pierre Bullet for the wealthy financier Antoine Crozat, who gave it to his son-in-law, the Comte d'Évreux. It later belonged to Louis-Antoine Crozat, Baron de Thiers, who filled the house with the magnificent collection of paintings brought together by his father and uncle; after his death in 1770, the collection was sold to Catherine II of Russia. Later owned by the Maréchal-Duc de Broglie, the house was occupied from 1826 to 1832 by successive presidents of the Chamber of Deputies, among them Royer-Collard, Casimir, Perier, and Laffitte. Now owned by the Credit Foncier.

* La Folie Saint-James
39, avenue de Madrid, Neuilly (see page 266)

* Hôtel de Galliffet
50, rue de Varenne (see page 110)

* Hôtel Gouffier de Thoix
56, rue de Varenne (see page 96)

Hôtel Gouthière
6, rue Pierre-Bullet

Built about 1780 by Métivier for the famous chaser and gilder of metalwork Pierre Gouthière, who had to sell the house about 1787. Especially fine are the courtyard façade, its forepart decorated with a bas-relief in the antique style, and the Pompeiian décor of the interior. Privately owned.

Hôtel de Guénégaud
60, rue des Archives

Built in 1648–51 by François Mansart, the house was redecorated inside in the early 18th century for the farmer-general Romanet. Sadly disfigured in the 19th century, it has recently been well restored and houses the Musée de la Chase ("Hunting Museum").

Hôtel de Guénégaud

Hôtel de Lamballe

Hôtel d'Hallwyl
28, rue Michel-le-Comte

Built in the early 18th century, the house was entirely remodeled in 1766 by Ledoux (this being his first important commission) for the Comte d'Hallwyl, colonel of the Swiss Guards regiment. It was later leased to the bank of Thélusson, Necker et Cie and served as the home of the banker Jacques Necker and his wife. It was here, in 1766, that their daughter, Madame de Staël, was born. The magnificent wainscoting was unfortunately removed by M. Guyot de Villeneuve to his town house in the Rue de Messine. The garden, surrounded by a peristyle in the antique manner, is covered over by ugly glass windows. Privately owned.

Hôtel d'Hénin
20, rue de Washington

Built about 1820 for the Princesse d'Hénin, this is an interesting example of Restoration architecture which still has a large part of its original interior décor. Owned by the Compagnie Française des Pétroles.

* Hôtel de Jarnac
8, rue Monsieur (see page 194)

Hôtel de Lamballe
16–20, avenue de Lamballe

After belonging to the Duc de Lauzun, husband of the Grande Mademoiselle, then brother-in-law of Saint-Simon, the house was remodeled in the late 18th century for the Princesse de Lamballe, superintendent of Marie-Antoinette's household. It was occupied in the 19th century by the nursing home of Dr. Blanche, where Gérard de Nerval was treated twice, in 1853 and 1854, and where Maupassant died in 1893. It is now occupied by the Turkish Embassy.

* Hôtel Lambert
2, rue Saint-Louis-en-l'Ile (see page 74)

Hôtel Le Hon

Hôtel de Lamoignon
24, rue Pavée

Built in 1594–98 for Diane de France, Duchesse d'Angoulême. A natural daughter of Henri II, she married first Orazio Farnese, Duke of Castro, then the Duc de Montmorency. The house later passed to the Lamoignon family. The novelist Alphonse Daudet lived there in the 1860s, during which time he wrote *Fromont jeune et Risler aîné* and *Jack*. Purchased by the city of Paris in 1928 and restored, it now houses the Bibliothèque Historique de la Ville de Paris.

* Hôtel de Lassay
128, rue de l'Université (see page 198)

* Hôtel Lauzun
17, quai d'Anjou (see page 64)

Hôtel Lebrun
49, rue du Cardinal-Lemoine

Built in 1700 by Boffrand for the nephew of the painter Charles Le Brun (or Lebrun), who here offered hospitality to Watteau. Owned by the city of Paris.

Hôtel Le Hon
9, rond-point des Champs-Elysées

Built under the Second Empire (1852–70) for the Comtesse Le Hon, wife of the Belgian Ambassador and mistress of the Duc de Morny. The Duke built himself a smaller house next door, known as *La Niche à Fidèle;* unfortunately this was recently demolished in order to enlarge the Hôtel Le Hon. The apartments, lavishly decorated in the Louis XV style, are occupied by the newspaper company Jours de France.

Hôtel Le Peletier de Saint-Fargeau
29, rue de Sévigné

Built by Pierre Bullet in 1686 for Le Peletier de Souzy. Here in the early 1790s lived the revolutionist Le Pe-

Hôtel Libéral Bruant

letier de Saint-Fargeau, who in January 1793 voted for the death of Louis XVI and was assassinated the next day in the Palais-Royal by a former member of the King's bodyguard. The fine wainscoting inside is still intact. Now part of the Bibliothèque Historique de la Ville de Paris.

HÔTEL LIBÉRAL BRUANT
1, rue de la Perle

Built for himself in 1685 by the architect Libéral Bruant, who also built the Invalides and the Salpêtrière. Later occupied by Guillaume de L'Hospital, a famous mathematician; then, at the end of the 18th century, by J. R. Perronet, who here set up the École des Ponts et Chaussées ("Civil Engineering School") which he had founded. Admirably restored, it houses today the Bricard Museum and its fine collection of metalwork.

* HÔTEL DE LUZY
6, rue Férou (see page 86)

MAISON DE BALZAC
47, rue Raynouard

This 18th-century house was originally the outbuilding, used as an orangery and theater, of a "folly" erected along the Rue Raynouard and now demolished. Balzac lived here from 1840 to 1847, while writing the latter part of his *Comédie humaine*. Owned by the city of Paris.

HÔTEL DE MAISONS
51, rue de l'Université

Designed by Lassurance and built in 1723 for François Duret, secretary of the Grand Conseil and "developer" of this neighborhood, who sold it in 1727 to the Président de Maisons. It was later owned by the Soyecourt, Saint-Aulaire, and Decaze families, before being acquired by Duke Pozzo di Borgo. The ground-floor rooms still have their fine original paneling, attributed to Le Roux. Privately owned.

HÔTEL MANSART DE SAGONNE
28, rue des Tournelles

Built for himself in 1667–70 by the great Jules Hardouin-Mansart, chief architect to Louis XIV and designer of the Hall of Mirrors at Versailles, the Grand Trianon, the Château de Marly, the Place Vendôme, the church of the Invalides, etc. The house was later occupied by the Duchesse de Mouchy, lady-in-waiting to Marie Leczinska, then by Marie-Antoinette before she became Queen. Of the original interior decorations of 1687–92, the ceiling paintings by Mignard and Lafosse survive, though in part hidden behind false ceilings. Privately owned.

HÔTEL DE MARLE
11, rue Payenne

Built in the early 17th century, the house was owned by Hercor de Marle, Seigneur de Versigny, then by the La Trémoille family, and next by Yolande de Polastron, future Duchesse de Polignac and favorite of Marie-Antoinette. Recently well restored, it houses the Institut Tessin.

HÔTEL DE MADEMOISELLE MARS
1, rue de la Tour-des-Dames

Originally known as the Hôtel de Bougainville, then as the Hôtel de Gouvion Saint-Cyr, it was acquired in 1824 by the famous actress Mademoiselle Mars, who had it remodeled by Visconti. It then passed to the Prince de Wagram. Inside survives a pretty sitting room decorated with arcades. Owned by La Concorde and occupied by the insurance company La Fédération Continentale.

HÔTEL DE MASSA
38, rue du Faubourg-Saint-Jacques

This house originally stood at the corner of the Champs-Elysées and the Rue La Boétie, but in 1928 it was removed stone by stone to its persesent site. Built in 1784 by the architect Le Boursier for Thiroux de Montsauge, it passed later to the Duc de Richelieu, then in 1830 to the Comte de Flahaut, father of the Duc de Morny. Owned by the Société des Gens de Lettres.

HÔTEL MASSERAN
11, rue Masseran

Built in 1787 by Brongniart for the Prince Des Masseran, descendant of an old Piedmontese family which had settled in Spain, who under the Empire was Spanish Ambassador to the court of Napoleon. Between World Wars I and II the house belonged to the Comte de Beaumont, a famous patron of the arts, who gave some sumptuous entertainments there and patronized the Ballets Russes, and the group of composers centering on Erik Satie known as Les Six, as well as Picasso, Jean Cocteau, and MarieLaurencin. Privately owned.

* HÔTEL MATIGNON
57, rue de Varenne (see page 116)

HÔTEL MERCY d'ARGENTEAU
16, boulevard Montmartre

Built in 1778 for the Austrian Ambassador in Paris, Florimund, Count Mercy d'Argenteau, whose correspondence with the Austrian Empress Maria-Theresa is a valuable record of life at the court of Louis XVI. The main floor still has its original décor of gilt paneling. Privately owned.

HÔTEL DE MIRAMION
47, quai de la Tournelle

Built in the 17th century for Madame de Miramion and occupied down to the French Revolution by the Filles de la Sainte-Famille, a charitable order founded by Madame de Miramion in 1661 and known after her as the Miramiones. Owned by the Pharmacie Centrale des Hôpitaux, which has opened here an interesting museum of pharmacy.

HÔTEL DE MONACO
57, rue Saint-Dominique

This was the masterpiece of the architect A. T. Brongniart, who built it in 1774–77 for Marie-Catherine de Brignoles, Princess of Monaco, separated from her husband and mistress of the Prince de Condé. Unfortunately the "embellishments" made about 1840 by the banker Hope disfigured the façades and eliminated all the 18th-century decorations, these being replaced by overwhelmingly lavish imitations. Later owned by the Prince de Sagan, who gave some splendid entertainments there. Occupied today by the Polish Embassy.

HÔTEL DE MONTESQUIOU
20, rue Monsieur

Built in 1781 by Brongniart for the Comte de Montesquiou, it passed in 1798 to his son, Grand Chamberlain to Napoleon I, whose wife ("Mama Quiou") was governess to Napoleon's only son, the so-called Roi de Rome. Purchased in 1851 by the Benedictine sisterhood of the Perpetual Adoration of the Holy Sacrament, the house was stripped of all its interior decora-

Maison de Balzac

Hôtel de Marle

Hôtel de Mlle Mars

Hôtel de Montesquiou

Hôtel de Rochechouart

tions. The novelist J. K. Huysmans lived here in 1901–02, in a small apartment on the courtyard (no longer in existence). Carefully restored, the house is now occupied by the Ministère de la Coopération.

HÔTEL DE MONTHOLON
23, boulevard Poissonnière

Built in 1775 by Soufflot Le Romain (nephew of the architect Germain Soufflot who built the Panthéon). The façade, adorned with a colossal order, is still very fine, in spite of the heightening and the shops that disfigure it. The first-floor drawing room still has its beautiful stucco decorations in the Pompeiian style. Privately owned.

HÔTEL DE MONTMOR
79, rue du Temple

Built in 1623 for Jean Habert de Montmor, treasurer at the Trésor de l'Epargne and thus, known as Montmor le Riche. His son, Henri Louis, a magistrate at the Parlement de Paris, gave hospitality here to Gassendi and founded a scientific society, known as the Académie Montmor, which in 1667 became the Academy of Sciences. Here Molière read his *Tartuffe* to a select company, after the performance of the play had been banned. The house was wholly remodeled in the 18th century. Privately owned.

* HÔTEL NISSIM DE CAMONDO
63, rue de Monceau (see page 244)

* HÔTEL DE NOIRMOUTIER
138, rue de Grenelle (see page 184)

* HOTEL DE PAÏVA
25, avenue des Champs-Élysées (see page 234)

* PALAIS DE L'ÉLYSÉE
55, rue du Faubourg-Saint-Honoré (see page 224)

PAVILLON DE BAGNOLET
148, rue de Bagnolet

Now part of the Hospice Debrousse, this house was built about 1720 for the Duchesse d'Orléans, wife of the Regent. It then stood in the ground of the Château de Bagnolet, which no longer exists.

PAVILLON CARRÉ DE BAUDOUIN
119, rue de Ménilmontant

Remodeled about 1770 by the architect Moreau-Desproux, this is a charming house in the Louis XVI style, with an Ionic peristyle and a fine garden in front. It is occupied by the Sisters of Charity of Saint Vincent de Paul.

* HÔTEL DE LA PRINCESSE MATHILDE
10, rue de Courcelles (see page 252)

Hôtel de Seignelay

HÔTEL DE PUSCHER
16, rue d'Auteuil

Built in the 17th century, this house was entirely remodeled in the 18th, probably around 1777, for the farmer-general Antoine Chardon, whose monogram figures in the pediment over the garden front. Owned by the École Saint-Jean of Passy.

HÔTEL DE ROCHECHOUART
110, rue de Grenelle

Built in 1776–77 for Madame de Courteilles by Mathurin Cherpitel (who also built the Hôtel du Châtelet). It passed to her daughter, the Marquise de Rochechouart, then to the Maréchal Augereau. Acquired by the government for the Ministry of National Education, which sill occupies it. The wainscoting in the large drawing room is among the finest of the Louis XVI period to be seen in Paris.

* HÔTEL DE ROHAN
87, rue Vieille-du-Temple (see page 18)

* HÔTEL DE ROQUELAURE
246, boulevard Saint-Germain (see page 144)

HÔTEL ROUSSEAU
66, rue La Rochefoucauld

Built in 1776 for himself by the architect Pierre Rousseau, who later designed the Hôtel de Salm, now the Palais de la Légion d'Honneur. Victor Hugo lived here from 1871 to 1874. Owned by the insurance company La Paternelle.

HÔTEL DE SAINT-AIGNAN
71, rue du Temple

This superb house was built between 1640 and 1650, to the designs of Le Muet, for Claude de Mesmes, Comte d'Avaux, who with Abel Servien was one of the chief French negotiators of the Treaty of Westphalia (1648). It was purchased in 1680 by the Comte de Saint-Aignan, later Duc de Beauvillier, who was the son-in-law of Colbert, a close friend of Saint-Simon, and tutor to the Duc de Bourgogne (heir to the throne, cut off by an early death). Now owned by the city of Paris, the house is being restored.

HÔTEL SAINT-FLORENTIN
2, rue Saint-Florentin

Built in 1767 by Jean Chalgrin for the Comte de Saint-Florentin, the house was purchased in 1811 by Talleyrand, who played host there to Czar Alexander I in 1814 and died there in 1838. Princess Lieven lived here in the 1840s and 1850s, holding a famous salon presided over the Buizot. Owned by the U.S. government and used by the American Embassy.

* HÔTEL DE SAINT-SIMON
128, boulevard Saint-Germain (see page 150)

HÔTEL SALÉ
5, rue de Thorigny

Built in 1656 for the tax-farmer Pierre Aubert de Fontenay. Owned from 1785 to 1788 by Monsignor de Juigné, Archbishop of Paris. Long occupied by the École des Métiers d'Art, it is now to house the future Picasso Museum. The staircase is one of the finest surviving examples of mid-17th-century French art, and several of the first-floor rooms will have their beautiful wainscoting of the Louis XV period.

* HÔTEL DE SALM
64, rue de Lille (see page 164)

* HÔTEL DE SALM-DYCK
97, rue du Bac (see page 156)

HÔTEL SARDINI
15, rue Scipion

Of the superb house built in 1565 for the wealthy Tuscan financier Scipione Sardini, nothing survives except for a charming arcaded gallery decorated with terrocotta medallions, which is now embodied in the later building that houses the central bakery of the Assistance Publique ("Poor Law Administration").

* HÔTEL SÉGUIER
16, rue Séguier (see page 160)

HÔTEL DE SEIGNELAY
80, rue de Lille

Like the neighboring Hôtel de Beauharnais, it was built by Boffrand in 1714. He sold it in 1718 to Charles-Éléonore Colbert, Comte de Seignelay and grandson of the great Colbert. Later owned by the Duc de Chârost and successively by the families of Sainte-Aldegonde, Cossé-Brissac, Lauriston, and Nicolai. The first-floor drawing room and boudoir still have their very fine original wainscoting. Occupied today by government offices.

* HÔTEL DE SENS
1, rue du Figuier (see page 14)

* HÔTEL DE SOUBISE
60, rue des Francs-Bourgeois (see page 30)

HÔTEL DE SOURDÉAC
8, rue Garancière

Built in 1646–48 for René de Rieux, Bishop of Léon, the house passed to his nephew, the Marquis de Sourdéac et d'Ouessant, who converted part of it into a theatre where, in the early 18th century, the great tragedienne Adrienne Lecouvreur made her début in the role of Pauline in Corneille's *Polyeucte*. Today owned and occupied by the publishing house Éditions Plon.

* HÔTEL SULLY
62, rue Saint-Antoine (see page 24)

HÔTEL DE TALLARD
78, rue des Archives

A notable example, among many others, of present-day vandalism: the gardens occupied by unsightly sheds, the staircase defaced by water seepage, the rooms sadly dilapidated. Built about 1650 by Pierre Bullet for Amelot de Chaillou, the house was acquired in 1712 by the Maréchal de Tallard. Privately owned.

HÔTEL TALMA
9, rue de la Tour-des-Dames

Here lived and died François-Joseph Talma (1763–1826), the greatest French actor of his day and a member of Napoleon's intimate circle. Privately owned.

HÔTEL DE TESSÉ
1, quai Voltaire

Its fine classical façade, decorated with Ionic pilasters, was erected in 1765 for the Comte de Tessé on the ruins of an earlier building. The first-floor apartment still has its fine Louis XVI woodwork, except for that of the large drawing room which is now in the Metropolitan Museum of Art, New York. Many well-known people lived in this house, among them Marshal Bugeaud, who died here of cholera in 1849.

* HÔTEL DE TOULOUSE
39, rue Croix-dex-Petits-Champs (see page 216)

Hôtel de Verrières

Hôtel Talma

HÔTEL TUBEUF
8, rue des Petits-Champs

Built in 1633 by Pierre Le Muet for the Président Tubeuf and then acquired by Cardinal Mazarin, who in 1644 commissioned François Mansart to add two superimposed galleries designed to house his magnificent collections. The building was enlarged in the early 18th century by the architect Robert de Cotte to house the Royal Library, which became the Bibliothèque Nationale, and was remodeled again in the 19th century by Henri Labrouste.

HÔTEL DE VAUDREUIL
7, rue de la Chaise

Built about 1765 and acquired in 1784 by the Comte de Vaudreuil, who brought together here a fine collection of paintings, part of which was purchased by Louis XVI and is now in the Louvre. Here, from 1803 to 1805, lived Napoleon's sister Elisa Bonaparte, and after 1809 Prince Aldobrandini, brother-in-law of Pauline Borghese, another of the Emperor's sisters. The house has recently been deprived of part of its garden and is now hemmed in by ghastly modern buildings.

HÔTEL DE VAUPALIÈRE
25, avenue Matignon

This fine house, built in 1775 by Colignon, has unfortunately lost most of its garden, and its courtyard façade is now dwarfed by recent buildings of no architectural interest. Privately owned.

HÔTEL DE VERRIÈRES
43–47, rue d'Auteuil

Built for an actress, Mademoiselle Antier, the house was later owned by Monsieur d'Épinay, who gave it to the Verrières sisters, both actresses, one of whom, Marie de Verrières, was the mistress of the Maréchal de Saxe and by him had a daughter who became the mother of George Sand. Remodeled at the end of the 18th century, the house is owned today by the Compagnie Française des Pétroles, which has built further offices in the grounds.

HÔTEL DE VILLETTE
27, quai Voltaire

A house famous for the fact that Voltaire, on his last visit to Paris, stayed here from February 5 to May 30, 1778, when he died in the apartment at the back of the courtyard. The house was then owned by the Marquis de Villette, who had married Voltaire's adopted daughter, Reine Philiberte de Varicourt—*Belle et Bonne*, as the old writer affectionately called her. The façade on the Seine was heightened and disfigured in the 19th century, but the first-floor drawing room remains as it was when Voltaire in his last days held court here. Privately owned.

Hôtel Tubeuf

Index of Art Works

Photo Credits